❦ FOLK ART NEEDLEPOINT ❦

CONTENTS

✳✳✳

INTRODUCTION

Tenui Filo Magnum Texitur Opus
"From one fine thread a work of art is born."

—*Dollfus-Mieg & Compagnie motto*

When it comes to needlepoint, I'm not out to slay dragons or change the world. Apart from cooking, I find that doing needlepoint is one of the more peaceful pastimes in my life. No politics are involved and relationships are neither made nor broken because of needlework; even budgets and schedules have little quarter here. For me, this centuries-old craft is all about private pleasures: I love deciding on a pattern, often tweaking it to make it even more personal for, say, my mother or goddaughter; and I make myself happily crazy dawdling over the vast array of colors and thread. I've been a hobby needle-pointer for more than a dozen years, and though there are times when I sew more avidly than others, my interest in needlepoint as an art form remains constant. For me, the historical relevance of a pattern is always of great interest, and no art form has deeper roots in our own soil than that of American folk art. Where better to look for pictorial examples that show us how people lived, their trade and means of livelihood, the celebration of birth or courtship and matrimony, the role of religion and faith, the honor bestowed upon the deceased. And yet despite the popularity of folk art among needlepointers, I couldn't find a book exclusively about American folk art motifs.

Thank goodness, then, for the American Folk Art Museum. I've long been enamored of the museum, and so I thought it would be the natural partner in developing patterns for a book on American folk art. The museum first opened its doors to the public in New York in 1961, and over these more than forty-five years its mission has greatly expanded. What began as a concentration of the American vernacular arts of the eighteenth and nineteenth centuries now includes works by self-taught artists in the twentieth and twenty-first centuries. Today, the museum's generous worldview encompasses the folk arts of Latin America, England, and parts of the European continent, among others, although it remains focused on folk art made in this country.

For *Folk Art Needlepoint*, I drew upon the museum's vast holdings and selected twenty objects upon which to develop needlework projects. I looked at furniture and carvings, weathervanes, frakturs, portraits, landscapes and still life, as well as textiles such as quilts and coverlets, hooked rugs, and samplers. The array of choices made for happy work. I was joined in this enterprise by Karyn Gerhard, and together we developed projects large and small, for the novice needle-pointer to the person with greater skills and capacity for more complex works. An eyeglass case and paperweight aren't difficult, nor is the fraktur-style picture frame, and yet I think even the experienced needlepointer could show off these works with pride. For greater challenge, there is a cushion depicting two cyclists as well as a sampler of an Arcadian landscape. Needlepoint is wonderful for the utility of its many applications, and so we offer such projects as a yard-long draft catcher that shows Manhattan, circa mid-1800s, and an elaborate foot-stool adapted from a stunning bed rug of 1806. I've organized the material into five groupings, which in themselves speak to folk art: daily life; birds, beasts, and bugs; flowers; hearts; and geometrics. All of the charts indicate the estimated skill level. Information about materials, stitches, and finishing, as well as conversion charts are in the back of the book. By way of offsetting the charts, photographs by Annie Schlechter of the completed projects in situ show the ease with which folk art needlepoint adapts to nearly any home décor. For those with an interest in our American heritage, detailed information is given for each of the works from the American Folk Art Museum. While this is not a big book, it's rich with ideas and wonderful art.

When most of us think about folk art, a world of simple beauty comes to mind. How nice that to partake of such modesty and appeal all you have to do is lift a finger—literally—and begin stitching, in and out, in and out.

Ruth Peltason

DAILY LIFE

CHAPTER 1

❋

❋

Reiter Family Album Quilt

Katie Friedman Reiter (1873–1942) and

Liebe Gross Friedman (dates unknown)

McKeesport, Pennsylvania; c. 1891–1892, reassembled 1976

Cotton and wool; 101 x 101" (256.5 x 256.5 cm)

Gift of Katherine Amelia Wine in honor of her grandmother

Theresa Reiter Gross and the makers of the quilt, her great-

grandmother Katie Friedman Reiter and her great-great-

grandmother Liebe Gross Friedman, and on behalf of a

generation of cousins: Sydney Howard Reiter, Penelope Breyer

Tarplin, Jonnie Breyer Stahl, Susan Reiter Blinn, Benjamin

Joseph Gross, and Leba Gross Wine, 2000.2.1

WELCOME FRIENDS DOOR HANGER

✴ ✴ ✴

The brightly colored cherries and pineapples of this little sign are actually taken from a mourning quilt and reworked into something hospitable and cheery. It hangs on a French door leading into a living room, though it can go just about anywhere, such as on a front door or bedroom door. A collection of marbleized pottery pig banks, circa mid-twentieth century, are an amusing addition atop the chest, which was made around 1850, and comes from the Bucks County area in Pennsylvania. The chest is a superb example of "cat's eye" painting. (Take a good look at the front of the chest and you'll see the "eyes.") In back is a Chinese oil painting on canvas, c. 1830, depicting *The Bark Lizzie* off Hong Kong.

MATERIALS

canvas: 12-gauge mono canvas, 12 x 12" (30.5 x 30.5 cm)

thread: DMC Pearl Cotton 3

needle: Size 20 tapestry

finished design: 7½ x 7½" (19 x 19 cm) (90 x 90 stitches)

stitches: Tent, Basketweave, Spiral Satin

skill level: Moderate

STITCHING

Begin with the decorative area using tent stitch, and then work the background in basketweave. To give the pineapples dimensionality, use a spiral satin stitch.

VARIATIONS

If you want this sign smaller, such as 5 x 5" (12.5 x 12.5 cm), use 18-gauge mono canvas (9 x 9") (23 x 23 cm) and DMC Pearl Cotton 5. If you prefer wool, use two of the three strands of Paternayan wool for the 12-gauge size and one strand for the 18-gauge size (see the conversion chart on page 142).

FINISHING

Although it's more common to use ribbon for hanging small signs and ornaments, I decided to use a bamboo purse handle because I thought that wood was more in keeping with the unpretentious nature of the motif. It's also less expected.

❋ ❋ ❋

COLOR		DMC PEARL	SKEINS
·	CREAM	712	4
+	MEDIUM GREEN AVOCADO	937	2
✖	MEDIUM YELLOW	3347	I
○	MEDIUM CHRISTMAS RED	304	I
▶	LIGHT GOLDEN BROWN	977	I

Mary H. Huntington

Attributed to Mary Way (1769–1833)

Brockton, Massachusetts; c. 1814

Watercolor and gouache on paper, in embossed

wallpaper-covered pasteboard box with silk lining and cotton padding;

3 x 2¹/₂ x 2³/₄" (7.5 x 5 x 7 cm) oval

Promised gift of Ralph Esmerian, P1.2001.4

SCROLL MOTIF PINCUSHION

✣ ✣ ✣

This darling pincushion was adapted from a miniature watercolor portrait of Mary Hallan Huntington, a child whose life was much too short (she died at the age of seven in 1820), but whose image remains timeless. Young Mary's likeness appears inside a handmade pasteboard box, which was covered in embossed wallpaper. The diminutive floral-like motif and double-scroll pattern of the wallpaper transfer perfectly as a design for the pincushion. And what rule says it must hold only *sewing* pins? Here, it's used for another kind of pin, in this case a Victorian mourning pin, a gold pin of English springer spaniels, and a brooch, c. 1910. An English thread box, mid-1800s, lends an air of authenticity.

MATERIALS

canvas: 18-gauge mono canvas, 7 x 9" (18 x 23 cm)

thread: DMC Cotton Floss

needle: Size 22 tapestry

finished design: 3 x 4¹⁄₄" (7.5 x 11 cm) (57 x 78 stitches)

stitches: Tent, Basketweave

skill level: Moderate

STITCHING

Use all six strands of the cotton floss. Begin with the decorative area using the tent stitch, and then work the background in basketweave.

VARIATIONS

If you prefer to work with wool, use one strand of Paternayan wool. You can easily adjust the shades of green to suit your own tastes if, for example, you lean toward cool blue-greens. Because this is a purely decorative design, you could choose completely different colors (maybe shades of brown or blue) or even set up something with greater contrast, such as a brown and red with an ecru background. Ideally, the colorways should be in the folk art palette.

FINISHING

The edging is really a tape of very small gold balls—a bit larger than seed pearls yet just as delicate in effect.

✳ ✳ ✳

COLOR		DMC FLOSS	SKEINS
▪	LIGHT PARROT GREEN	907	I
C	MEDIUM PARROT GREEN	906	I
▪	BLACK AVOCADO GREEN	934	3

Close Finish Hooked Rug

Artist unidentified

United States; early twentieth century

Wool and burlap with cotton binding; 32½ x 46" (82.5 x 117 cm)

Bequest of Gertrude Schweitzer, 1990.28.2

CLOSE FINISH CUSHION

"YOU'LL LOOK SWEET UPON THE SEAT OF A BICYCLE MADE FOR TWO . . ."—*from "Daisy Bell," lyrics by Harry Dacre, 1892*

By the time this hooked rug of two gentlemen cyclists, above, was made, bicycling had already become a national pastime in America, and bicycling clubs were in full swing, offering their members touring and racing activities. The bike depicted here was "the ordinary," more commonly known as the high wheeler. Although the overly large front wheel allowed the cyclist to go farther with one revolution of the tire, there was a significant downside: the high seat and disproportionate build meant that the rider nearly always toppled whenever making a sudden stop. But necessity is the mother of invention, and soon the bicycle went on to a more sensible distribution of weight and an allover easier ride. (In fact, the bicycle offered women a new-found freedom, leading Susan B. Anthony to famously declare in 1896 that "the bicycle has done more for the emancipation of women than anything else in the world.")

These earnest cyclists coast along with the paisley club chair in this sitting room. Although barely visible here, the fabric backing of the cushion is a charcoal gray-and-white wool menswear plaid, which keeps the overall application fairly neutral. In and among the books are a number of folk art pieces, including an English commemorative pitcher, c. 1790, with polychrome transfer-painted decoration and oval portraits depicting Samuel Adams and John Hancock; a painted leather fire bucket, c. 1830; and a New Hampshire wood carving in the form of a horse and seated rider, c. 1885. (The fire bucket would have been kept in a front hall in case of fire.)

The general sporty theme of the cushion also suggests a natural fit in a mudroom, among the usual pileup of sports equipment and other athletic gear. Don't have a mudroom? Don't despair. This cheery cushion is even at home in a child's bedroom.

MATERIALS

canvas: 12-gauge mono canvas, 20 x 15" (51 x 38 cm)

thread: Paternayan wool

needle: Size 20 tapestry

finished design: 15³/₄ x 11" (40 x 28 cm) (189 x 132 stitches)

stitches: Tent, Basketweave

skill level: Difficult

STITCHING

To lessen the appearance of any show-through, use a
brown or dark-colored canvas. Separate the wool strands
and use two of the three strands to stitch the project.
Begin with the decorative areas using the tent stitch, and
then work the larger areas of color in basketweave.

VARIATIONS

This pattern can also be worked as a footstool. Before
working the pattern, get a template for a footstool cushion
from your upholsterer or modify this project based on the
Packard Footstool on page 68 in the Flowers chapter. If the
pattern needs to be adjusted to fit the template, the easiest
way to do this is to either increase or decrease the number
of rows in the outer border.

FINISHING

In keeping with the use of wool yarn and to underscore the
sports motif, I chose a wool menswear fabric. The open
plaid is a classic pattern, resulting in just the right amount
of contrast with the nuanced colors in the background of
the canvas. The self-welt underscores the simplicity of the
finishing. Because of the menswear fabric, the pillow would
work equally well in a den or home office.

✳ ✳ ✳

COLOR		PATERNAYAN	SKEINS
◩	DARK BROWN GRAY	102	2
▣	VERY LIGHT ASH GRAY	101	2
▭	MEDIUM BROWN	411	1
⊥	LIGHT MOCHA BEIGE	464	4
~	LIGHT BEIGE BROWN	463	4
✕	LIGHT DESERT SAND	875	1
◎	LIGHT OLD GOLD	734	1
◔	MEDIUM TOPAZ	732	1
r	ULTRA VERY LIGHT BEIGE BROWN	842	1
◉	VERY LIGHT BEIGE BROWN	465	2
⊠	LIGHT SHELL GRAY	203	1
ф	DARK PEWTER GRAY	200	3
◖	BLACK	220	1
0	LIGHT BABY BLUE	505	1
◕	DARK BABY BLUE	503	1
◯	ULTRA VERY DARK BABY BLUE	551	1
◣	GARNET	900	1
◙	MEDIUM CORAL	842	1
◗	DARK ANTIQUE MAUVE	921	1
▣	MEDIUM CHRISTMAS RED	968	1
▣	WHITE	262	1
▪	202 BLENDED WITH 200	202	3
◉	202 BLENDED WITH 220		

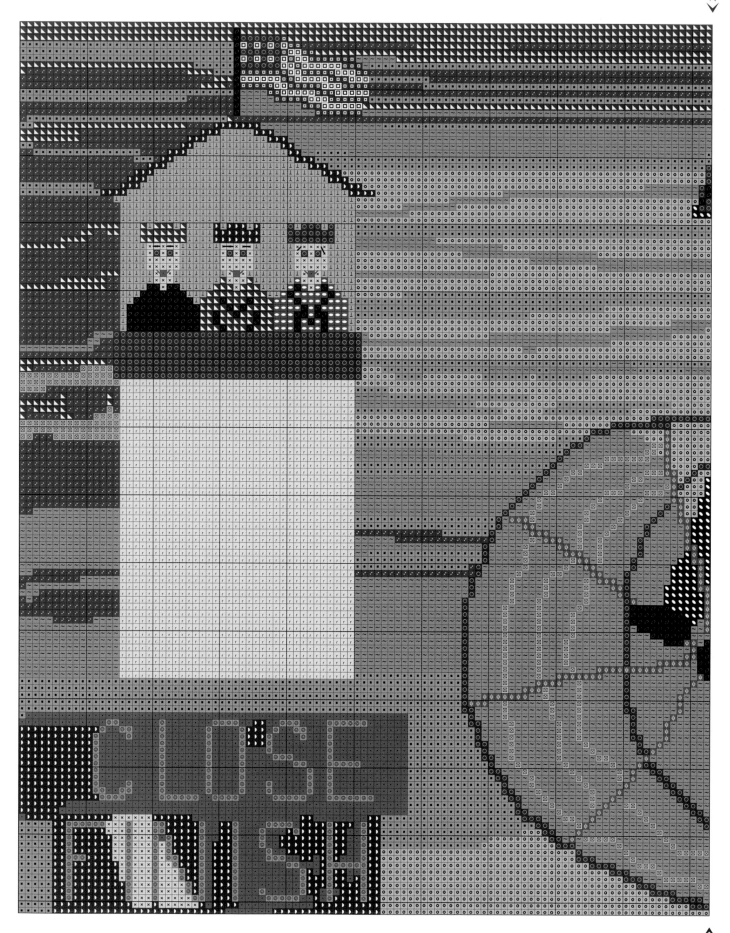

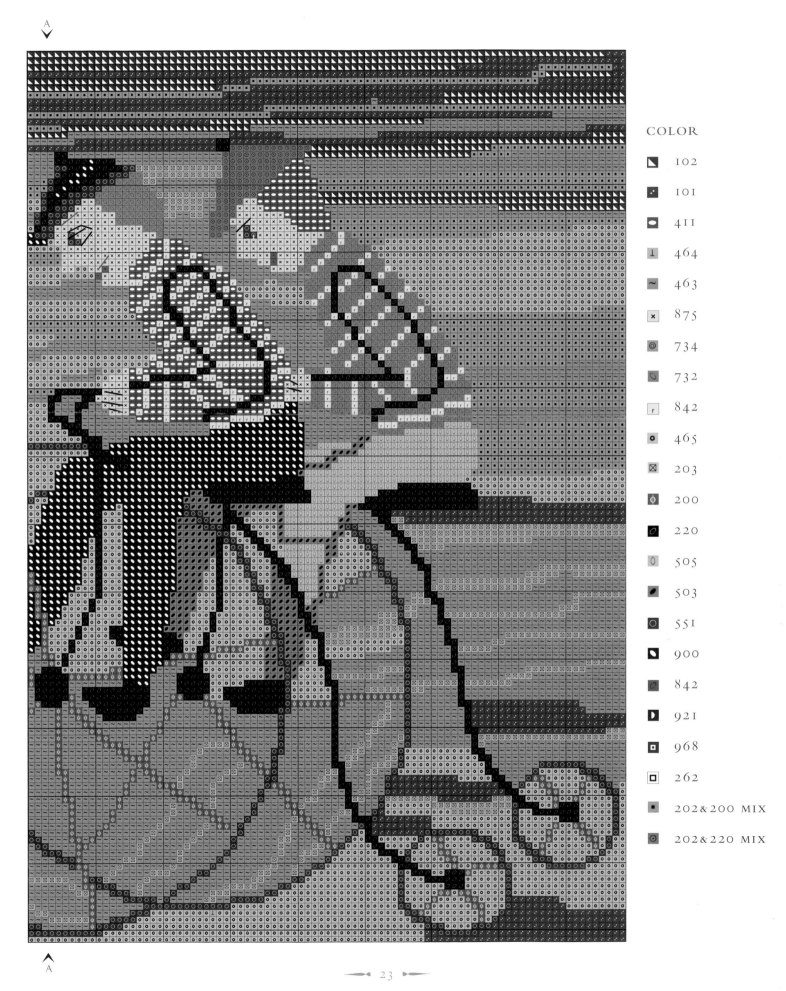

◣	102
⋮	101
⬯	411
⊥	464
~	463
×	875
◎	734
⟳	732
r	842
⊙	465
⊠	203
φ	200
⬭	220
◊	505
◗	503
○	551
◣	900
⟲	842
◖	921
▫	968
▫	262
▪	202 & 200 MIX
◉	202 & 220 MIX

SITUATION OF AMERICA, 1848.

Situation of America, 1848.

Artist unidentified

New York; 1848

Oil on wood panel; 34 x 57 x 1³/₈" (86 x 145 x 3.5 cm)

Promised gift of Ralph Esmerian, P1.2001.58

NEW YORK CITY DRAFT CATCHER

✳ ✳ ✳

A perfect trivia question: What city is depicted in this building tableau? Even if you are familiar with the architectural history of New York City, you might not recognize this view of the city as seen from Brooklyn in the mid-1800s. Understandably, this brightly colored draft catcher is meant to provide the household duty of blocking breezes and such when tucked into a windowsill or at the base of a door, but we couldn't resist the fun of positioning it on the couch. Here, the sky-blue velvet seems a natural surround for this yard-long pillow, where it has pride of place beneath a collection of English book jackets by novelist Elizabeth Bowen. Originally published in Great Britain in the 1930s and 1940s, the book jacket designs were wood engravings commissioned from artist Joan Hassall.

The rest of the art displays a home-spun collection of images of man's best friend. The inscription on the photograph of the poodle reads "Monsieur Bardot, 1963," which was perhaps the photographer's tongue-in-cheek reference to French actress Brigitte Bardot, who was very much the cat's meow at the time.

But back to the draft catcher for a moment: who says you can't put your draft catcher where you want? After all, it's your home.

MATERIALS

canvas: 14-gauge mono canvas, 42 x 9" (106.5 x 23 cm)

thread: Paternayan wool

needle: Size 20 tapestry

finished design: 36 x 3½" (91 x 9 cm) (49 x 504 stitches)

stitches: Tent, Basketweave

skill level: Difficult

STITCHING

Separate the wool strands and use two of the three strands. Begin with the decorative areas using tent stitch, and then work the larger areas of color in basketweave.

FINISHING

The repeat of the houses is so charming and lively that the fabric and trim are best kept low-key. If you intend to use this as a traditional draft catcher, you will want to select an upholstery-weight fabric that will stand up to wear. Although I picked a pattern of little birds in a blue sky to play off the houses, a dark solid is a smart way to camouflage dirt and dust. The trim is just a thin, dark brown cord. We considered having this made as a wedge shape, but in the end the box works wonderfully well. Sometimes a decision is really a matter of preference, neither right nor wrong.

COLOR		PATERNAYAN	SKEIN
·	LIGHT GRAY GREEN	515	7
⬛	BLACK	220	3
✖	BRICK RED	850	2
◔	LIGHT SHELL GRAY	203	I
▶	VERY DARK COFFEE BROWN	430	2
C	ECRU	262	2
▲	VERY DARK PISTACHIO GREEN	600	2
◉	MEDIUM BROWN	411	I

COLOR		PATERNAYAN	SKEIN
▼	LIGHT NAVY BLUE	502	I
▪	MEDIUM MOCHA BROWN	464	I
●	MEDIUM TOPAZ	732	I
◎	WHITE	260	2
◆	TAN	417	I
◻	LIGHT BROWN	412	I
▽	DARK PEWTER GRAY	200	I
◡	LIGHT BEIGE BROWN	465	I

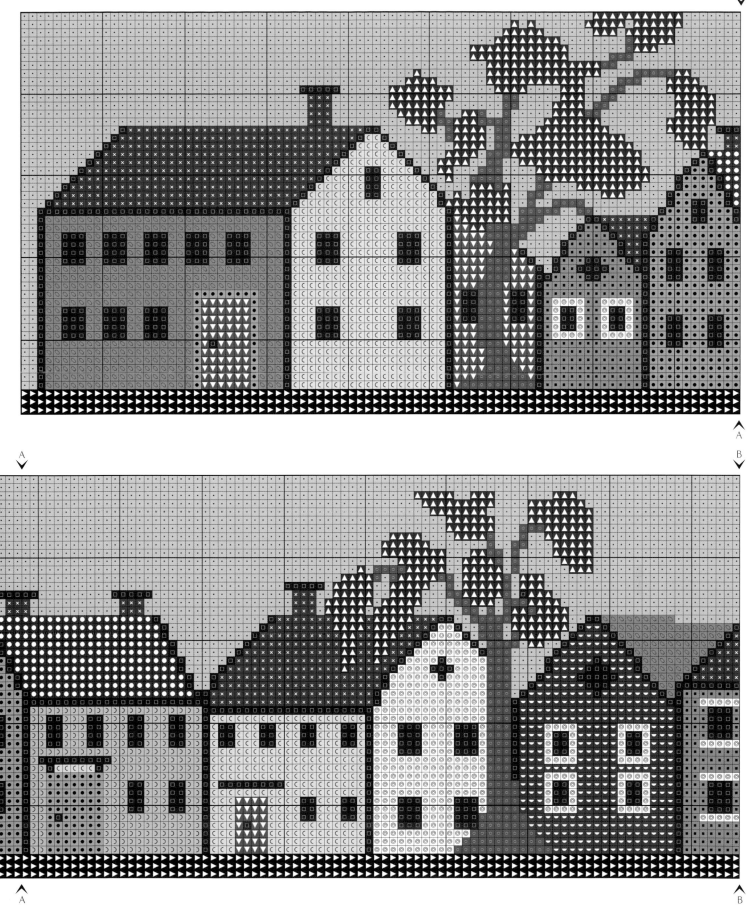

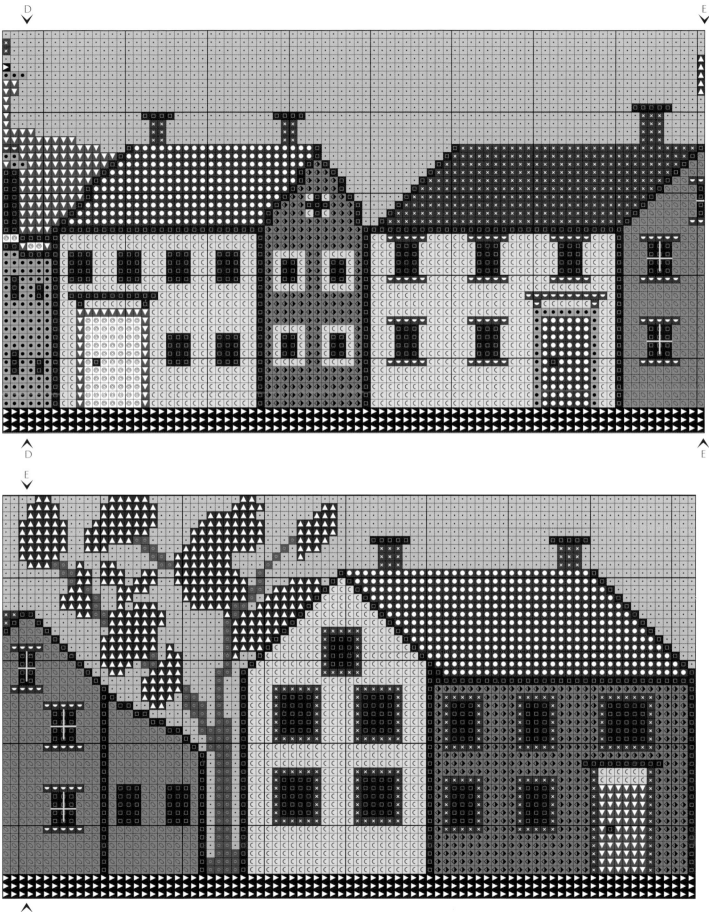

Horse and Rider Weathervane

Artist unidentified

New England; c. 1870

Cast iron with traces of paint; 22⅛ x 42½ x 1" (56 x 108 x 2.5 cm)

Promised gift of Ralph Esmerian, P1.2001.328

WEATHERVANE SILHOUETTE

❋ ❋ ❋

You say tomāto, we say tomäto; you say stark, we say simplicity. Sometimes the choice of where to place something is not about adding, but about taking away, making little rest stops for the eye.

The graphic contours of this weathervane—an acrobatic figure, spear at the ready, astride a horse in full gallop—in the black Dutch-style frame is a quiet fit above the Windsor chair, whose rails against the wall continue the black-and-white palette of this vignette. The sampler, partially seen above the finished needlepoint piece, at top, was made in Pennsylvania in 1827.

MATERIALS

canvas: 17-gauge mono canvas, 15 x 12" (38 x 30.5 cm)

thread: DMC Cotton Floss

needle: Size 22 tapestry

finished design: 11 x 7¼" (28 x 18.5 cm) (153 x 101 stitches)

stitches: Tent, Basketweave, Reverse Checkerboard

skill level: Easy

STITCHING

Use all six strands of the cotton floss to work this project. For the background, combine three strands of white and three strands of ecru. The piece should be stitched as follows: First do the border in tent stitch, then work the horse and rider in basketweave (the border will be useful as a guide to check the positioning of the horse when you stitch). Finish the background in a reverse checkerboard.

VARIATIONS

If you want, you can stitch the background entirely in basketweave. This piece can be worked as either a hanging piece of art or a cushion. Instructions for adapting either idea are on page 141.

FINISHING

To complement the silhouette and to maintain the graphic nature of the work, I chose a Dutch-style ebony wood frame.

❉ ❉ ❉

COLOR	DMC FLOSS	SKEINS
☐ WHITE	BLANC	7
◨ ECRU	ECRU	5
◼ VERY DARK ROYAL BLUE	820	2
✕ BLACK	310	3

BIRDS, BEASTS & BUGS

CHAPTER 2

⁂

⁂

Appliquéd Carpet

Artist unidentified

Northeastern United States, possibly Maine; c. 1860

Wool appliqué and embroidery on wool;

112 x 158" (284.5 x 401.5 cm)

Promised gift of Ralph Esmerian, P1.2001.294

WOODLAND
PAPERWEIGHT

❋ ❋ ❋

"If a cluttered desk is a sign of a cluttered mind, of what, then, is an empty desk?" remarked the über-brilliant Albert Einstein. Yet for all we know, even Einstein had a paperweight or two on his desk. With its bosky scene of delicate butterflies and birds, this charming paperweight won't cramp the formation of any genius thoughts, but it will add a touch of tidiness and order. An assortment of books from the series Our Friend the Dog, edited by Rowland Johns, c. 1930s, is stacked alongside a mid-century glass-and-metal inkwell and pen holder and turn-of-the-nineteenth-century octagonal creamware plate with the inscription "Present for writing well."

MATERIALS

canvas: 16-gauge mono canvas, 12 x 9" (30.5 x 23 cm)

thread: DMC Pearl Cotton 5

needle: Size 22 tapestry

finished design: 6 x 3" (15 x 7.5 cm) (97 x 48 stitches)

stitches: Tent, Basketweave

skill level: Easy

STITCHING

To lessen the appearance of any show-through, use a brown or dark-colored canvas. Begin with the decorative areas using tent stitch, and then work the background in basketweave.

VARIATIONS

This is a straightforward project that lends itself to a couple easy tweaks, still in the blue palette. For example, you can change the background color to a rich French marine blue, such as 979, or a bright blue, such as 826. Or you can flip the colors already in the pattern and make the birds navy blue (336) and the background light baby blue (3325).

FINISHING

This is a simple project—it's easy to stitch and since it won't receive much wear, select a fabric that offers enough resistance so that the filling doesn't cause any unseemly lumps. I chose a dark navy with small off-white polka dots because I like the tension between elements that are figural (the design on the front) and geometric. Anything too busy would have detracted from the little woodland scene. I kept the trim simple but pretty: our finisher actually made the little cord in my favorite shade of blue.

Instead of using this as a paperweight, you can fill this with dried flowers such as lavender or roses, or herbs such as chamomile, mint, or even rosemary for something less expected, and use it as a sachet. Some herb and spice shops carry fragrance beads (think vanilla or morning rain), which are very potent. If you decide to use these, only a $^{1}/_{2}$ teaspoon at most is needed; pad out the balance of the filling with rice or dried beans.

COLOR		DMC PEARL	SKEINS
	MEDIUM PISTACHIO GREEN	320	1
	LIGHT BABY BLUE	3325	1
	MEDIUM BABY BLUE	334	1
	NAVY BLUE	336	1
	VERY LIGHT TERRA COTTA	758	1
	MEDIUM TERRA COTTA	356	1
	OFF-WHITE	746	1
	VERY LIGHT BROWN	435	1
	DARK COFFEE BROWN	801	1
	MEDIUM GARNET	815	1

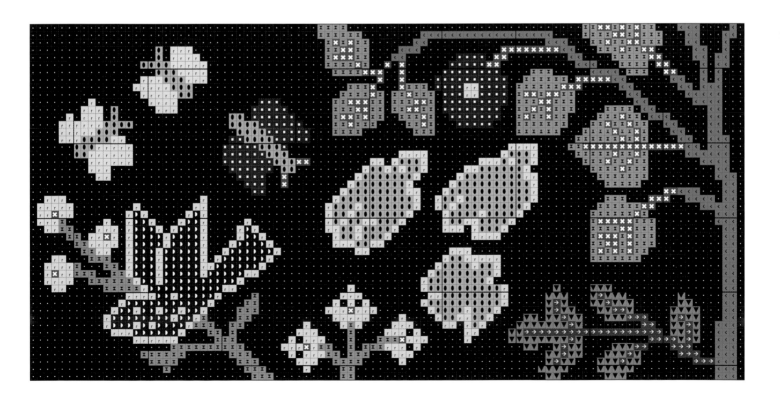

Hannah Carter Canvaswork Picture

Hannah Carter (dates unknown)

Boston; c. 1748

Silk and wool on fine linen; 21¹/₁₆ x 18⁷/₈" (53.5 x 48 cm)

Promised gift of Ralph Esmerian, P1.2001.279

HANNAH CARTER TAPESTRY

"LOVE IS LIKE A BUTTERFLY: IT GOES WHERE IT PLEASES AND IT PLEASES WHERE IT GOES."—Author Unknown

No wonder Thoreau was content to sit at Walden Pond, for a pastoral setting is a charmed life where nature is at its most abundant and most tolerant and all creatures are in harmony and at peace with one another. In this needlework vignette, birds sing, sheep roam freely, and plants are in full flower; famine and warfare have no quarter here. It's often remarked that young people are natural optimists. That would seem true of the girl who made this remarkable needlework, with its keen sense of scale and perspective, done when she was only sixteen and at boarding school in Boston. Our facsimile version rests on a dining chair, c. 1830, below a mahogany shelf holding a few treasured porcelain figurines.

MATERIALS

canvas: 14-gauge mono canvas, 19 x 21" (48.5 x 53.5 cm)

thread: DMC Cotton Floss

needle: Size 20 tapestry

finished design: 13¼ x 15¼" (33.5 x 38.5 cm)

(184 x 214 stitches)

stitches: Tent, Basketweave

skill level: Difficult

STITCHING

Use all six strands of the floss to stitch the project. To lessen the appearance of any show-through, use a brown or dark-colored canvas. Work the decorative areas in tent stitch (it is easiest to begin with the girl's dress and go from there); then stitch the larger areas, including the background, in basketweave.

VARIATIONS

Because this is a facsimile of a sampler made in 1748, it's best to keep the design and colors as they are.

FINISHING

I think this is the most "authentic" of the projects adapted from the American Folk Art Museum, and for that reason initially I wanted the look of a period frame. My instinct was to use a reddish-brown frame with minimal articulation, but the result was a bit plain; then I went the other direction and considered a weathered wood frame with pale reddish stenciling of leaves and such, which looked fantastic: it was so over the top that it actually heightened the colorful needlework. But I shied away, for it seemed too specific. Ultimately, I went with a silvered frame, with red highlights, which I thought was more broadly suited to modern home décors. As you can see, there are many options when it comes to framing.

COLOR		DMC FLOSS	SKEINS
◨	BLACK	310	I
⌒	VERY LIGHT GRAY GREEN	928	3
◒	SKY BLUE	519	I
▫	DARK TURQUOISE	3810	12
◡	VERY DARK TURQUOISE	3809	4
◖	VERY DARK GRAY GREEN	924	5
◑	CHRISTMAS RED	321	I
▪	MEDIUM CORAL	350	2
◎	CORAL	351	2
♥	LIGHT CORAL	352	2
○	PEACH	353	2
◆	OFF-WHITE	746	2
▫	LIGHT TAWNY	951	I
◫	VERY LIGHT BEIGE BROWN	842	I
▪	VERY LIGHT TAN	738	I
■	LIGHT TAN	437	I
▼	LIGHT DESERT SAND	950	2
▣	DARK DESERT SAND	3772	3
◉	VERY DARK DESERT SAND	632	I
▢	GOLDEN BROWN	3826	I
◈	DARK KHAKI GREEN	3011	I
◐	MEDIUM KHAKI GREEN	3012	3
▲	LIGHT KHAKI GREEN	3013	4

Bird of Paradise Quilt Top

Artist unidentified

Vicinity of Albany, New York; 1858–1863

Cotton, wool, silk, and ink with silk embroidery;

84$\frac{1}{2}$ x 69$\frac{5}{8}$" (214.5 x 177 cm)

Gift of the Trustees of the American Folk Art

Museum, 1979.7.1

BIRD OF PARADISE
WEDGE PILLOW

✳ ✳ ✳

It would be surprising if the great American poet Wallace Stevens had ever seen this Bird of Paradise folk art design, yet the majestic line from his poem "Of Mere Being," written in 1954, nearly a hundred years after this quilt top was made, seems an apt description of the design: "The bird's fire-fangled feathers dangle down."

The pillow wedge adds a burst of brightness in this softly colored bedroom, although there is a touch of wit in the toile-covered headboard—it's actually a play on a famous photograph taken by *Life* photographer Dean Loomis in 1957, ten years after the debut of Christian Dior's all-important launch of the New Look in 1947.

MATERIALS

canvas: 12-gauge mono canvas, 26 x 21" (66 x 53.5 cm)

thread: DMC Pearl Cotton 3

needle: Size 20 tapestry

finished design: 20 x 15" (51 x 38 cm) (240 x 180 stitches)

stitches: Tent, Basketweave, Byzantine

skill level: Moderate

STITCHING

Begin by stitching the bird, starting with the tail, in basketweave. Do the branch and other decorative areas using tent stitch. Switch over to basketweave for the larger areas of the bird. Finish with the background in Byzantine stitch.

VARIATIONS

The easiest way to vary this is to make the background in a color other than this sunny yellow. Before changing the color, first decide in what room you will want the pillow and choose a background color to work with the décor.

If you prefer to have a less decorative or textured background, you can use basketweave instead.

FINISHING

Because the American Folk Art Museum's Bird of Paradise is so exuberantly colored, I decided to match it with a rich damask, a fairly traditional textile, and tricolored trim. With this sort of design, you really can go either way—ultra simple or more richly textured, as shown here. Damask textiles were often used for bedding and table linens in the nineteenth and twentieth centuries. Although damask originally came from areas in China and India, by the twelfth century it was prevalent in Damascus such that its modern name came from this Syrian town. Damask is particularly effective for embellished patterns, as in the fabric I chose, as well as for pastoral scenes of birds or flowers or geometric forms such as the Greek key pattern. The trim, which has dashes of red, blue, and green, accentuates the bird's tail feathers.

COLOR		DMC PEARL	SKEINS
▲	DARK GARNET	814	2
✚	VERY DARK BEIGE BROWN	838	2
▨	VERY DARK DESERT SAND	632	2
◼	BLACK	310	1
◇	MEDIUM BABY BLUE	334	1
◼	DARK PEACOCK BLUE	806	1
·	VERY PALE YELLOW	3823	12
⊙	CREAM	712	2
⬭	LIGHT KHAKI GREEN	3013	2
⬤	DARK KHAKI GREEN	3011	1
◾	AVOCADO GREEN	469	2
◨	CHRISTMAS RED	321	3
◪	ROSE	335	1
◻	MEDIUM OLD GOLD	729	1

▲	814	◈	334	⊙	712	◗	321
✚	838	•	806	⊘	3013	⊘	335
▨	632	·	3823	⏀	3011	▪	729
◪	310			▪	469		

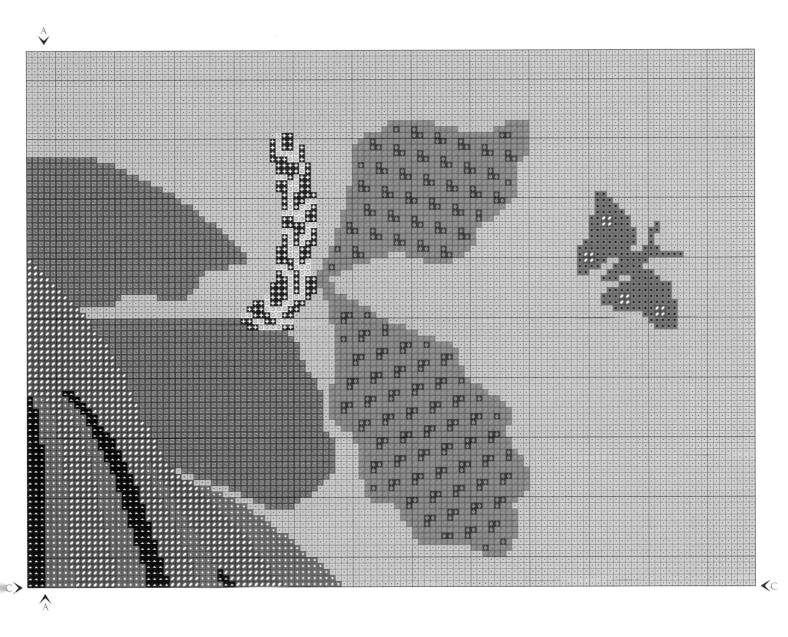

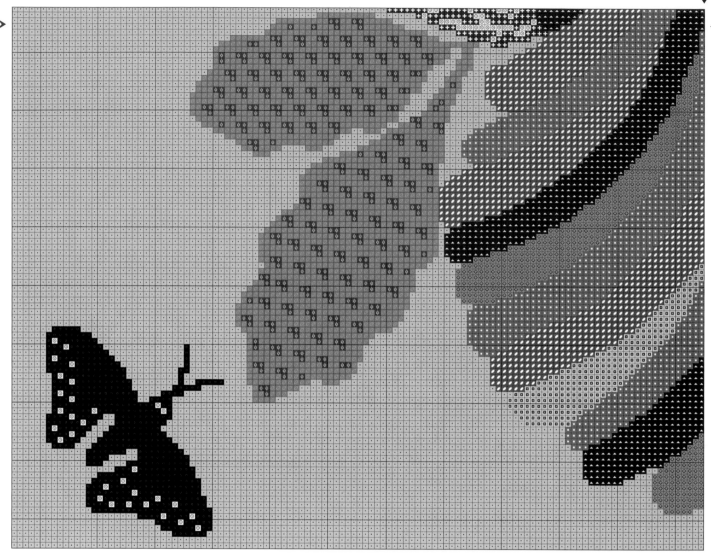

▲	814	◇	334	⊙	712	◢	321
✚	838	•	806	⦰	3013	◩	335
▨	632	·	3823	φ	3011	▪	729
⊙	310			▪	469		

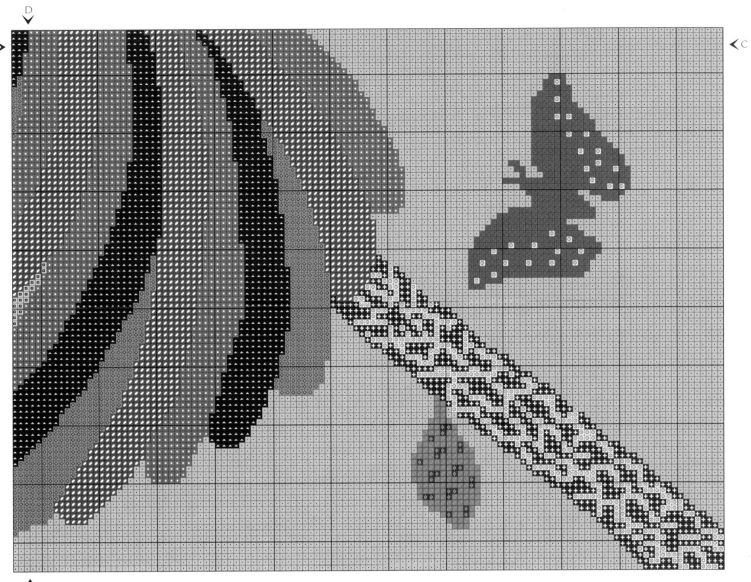

FLOWERS

CHAPTER 3

✳

✳

Cross River Album Quilt

Mrs. Eldad Miller (1805–1874) and others

Cross River, New York; 1861

Cotton and silk with wool embroidery;

90 x 75" (229 x 190.5 cm)

Gift of Dr. Stanley and Jacqueline Schneider, 1980.8.1

CROSS RIVER CUSHION

✳ ✳ ✳

It may look like a step back in time, but actually this is a home where folk art is expressed just about everywhere, resulting in vignettes as handsome and tasteful as this foyer, anchored by the portrait of an unidentified gentleman, c. 1835, Vermont, attributed to the painter Asahel Powers. Other features are the Boston bowback Windsor chair, c. 1790, with the Cross River Cushion, weathered bench and dainty shorebird, and hand-stenciled swag border.

MATERIALS

canvas: 12-gauge mono canvas, 18 x 18" (45.5 x 45.5 cm)

thread: Anchor wool

needle: Size 20 tapestry

finished design: 14 x 14" (35.5 x 35.5 cm) (168 x 168 stitches)

stitches: Tent, Basketweave

skill level: Moderate

STITCHING

Begin with the decorative areas using tent stitch, and then work the background in basketweave.

VARIATIONS

For a smaller cushion, work the pattern on 14-gauge mono canvas, which will produce a 12 x 12" (30.5 x 30.5 cm) cushion.

FINISHING

Dictionary definitions of ticking tend to describe it as a strong cotton or linen fabric, most often used for pillows and mattresses, but that only speaks to the most antiseptic way of understanding the evergreen appeal of ticking. Also known as pillow ticking, the telltale stripes and cream background now come in many different colors, although navy, black, and brown are more traditionally seen. Because of the strong graphics in this pillow, I immediately thought of using a ticking and decided to play it up a bit by contrasting the black ticking on the back with a welt made of red ticking. This is a case of turning up the volume, so to speak, but only a little. You might prefer to work with a solid covered fabric, which is a safe choice; if you want a pattern, take care not to overwhelm the impact of the graphic design.

COLOR		ANCHOR	SKEINS
☐	CREAM	8292	15
◠	GREEN	9178	4
▣	RED	8218	6
▫	COPPER	921	2
◉	BLACK	9666	4

Centennial Quilt

Possibly Gertrude Knappenberger (dates unknown)

Possibly Emmaus, Pennsylvania; 1876

Cotton with cotton embroidery; 84 x 74" (213 x 188 cm)

Gift of Rhea Goodman, 1979.9.1

PENNSYLVANIA GERMAN CURTAIN TIEBACK

"OH, WHAT A BEAUTIFUL MORNIN'! OH WHAT A BEAUTIFUL DAY!"—*from "Oh, What a Beautiful Mornin'!" by Rodgers and Hammerstein*

Happiness is sunlight and a pretty room. The raspberry-and-cream silk stripe curtain (remember striped taffy?) is a flattering foil for the decorative floral tieback. Though the other bits seen here— the watercolor of a butterfly by textile designer Vera and the little oil of some hunting dogs—differ in time and style, they contribute to the overall color scheme of soft reds and bright turquoise. Nothing is matchy-matchy stylistically, which is exactly the point: trust in your favorite things to "speak" to one another and naturally form their own dialogue. It usually works.

MATERIALS

canvas: 14-gauge mono canvas, 8 x 33" (20.5 x 84 cm)

thread: DMC Pearl Cotton 3

needle: Size 20 tapestry

finished design: 3¼ x 28" (8 x 71 cm) (46 x 395 stitches)

stitches: Tent, Basketweave

skill level: Moderate

STITCHING

Begin with the decorative areas using tent stitch, and then work the background in basketweave.

VARIATIONS

The yarn amounts given are for one curtain tieback; if you are making a pair, simply double the amount of yarn indicated. Alternatively, this can be used for something called a bell pull. Frankly, I think bell pulls are outdated (they remind me of scenes from *The Magnificent Ambersons*, 1942), so I would only use this as a curtain tieback. Also, it seems to beg the question: for whom does the bell pull?

FINISHING

This is so pretty, and because it enhances a curtain, common sense dictated the choice of a neutral fabric and trim. Using an off-white or ivory and mocha gimp needn't seem a cop-out, but a smart way to know when simple is sublime.

✳ ✳ ✳

COLOR		DMC PEARL	SKEINS
			(for one tieback)
·	CREAM	712	11
⌒	DARK CRANBERRY	601	1
◖	VERY DARK CRANBERRY	600	1
✕	LIGHT PEWTER	169	2
⌗	MEDIUM AVOCADO GREEN	937	1
⊘	MEDIUM TANGERINE	741	1
◗	LIGHT BEIGE BROWN	841	1
◪	VERY DARK DESERT SAND	632	1
◈	VERY DARK BEIGE BROWN	838	1

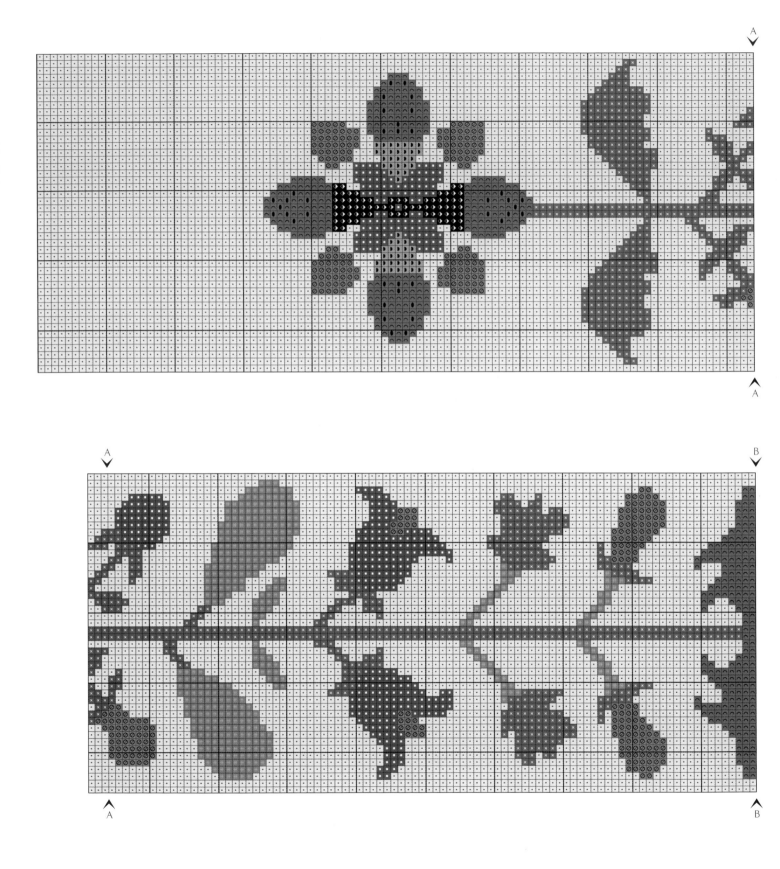

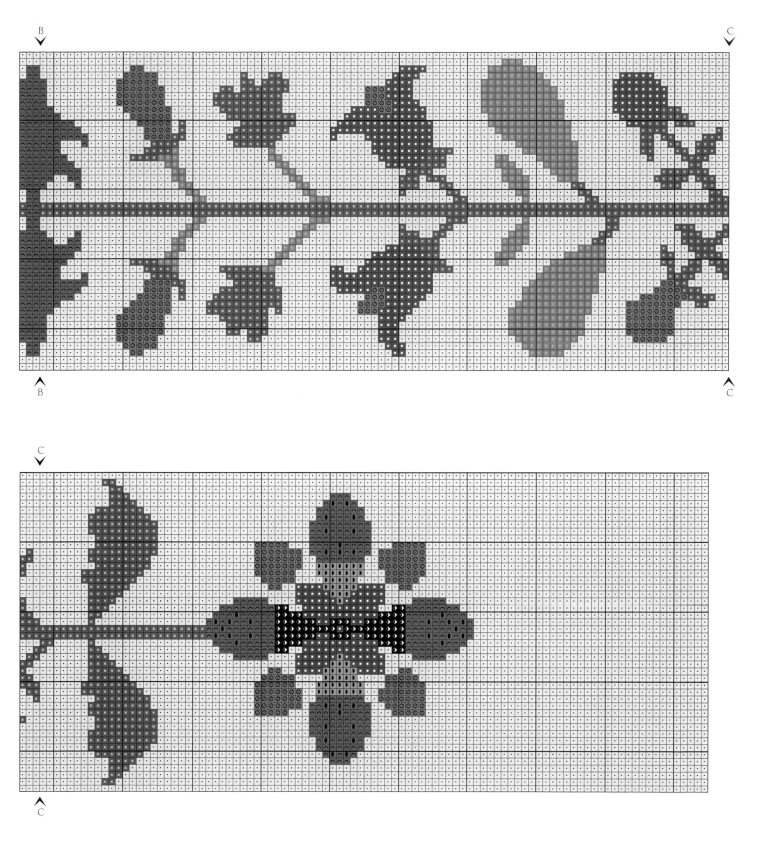

Packard Bed Rug
Packard family member
Jericho, Vermont; 1806
Wool; 94 x 90½" (239 x 230 cm)
Gift of Cyril Irwin Nelson in honor of
Cary Forney Baker Jr., 2002.31.1

PACKARD FOOTSTOOL

✳ ✳ ✳

Earth colors always go together—you can't go wrong with shades of brown and red, in this case accented by deeply rich blues. The outstanding feature here is the pine fire board, c. 1840, with an oval landscape depicting Saco, Maine. The owner of a fire board as appealing as this one was indeed fortunate, for in the warm summer months fire boards were used to cover the fireplace and keep out drafts. The child-size Windsor side chair, c. 1830, is in keeping with the New England theme, as is the footstool with the turned legs, a faithful reproduction of an early nineteenth-century one found in upstate New York.

MATERIALS

canvas: 12-gauge mono canvas, 25 x 22" (63.5 x 56 cm)

thread: Paternayan wool

needle: Size 20 tapestry

finished design: 18¹/₂ x 15¹/₄" (47 x 38.5 cm)

(222 x 183 stitches)

stitches: Tent, Basketweave

skill level: Difficult

STITCHING

To lessen the appearance of any show-through, use a brown or dark-colored canvas. Separate the strands of wool and use two of the three strands to stitch the project. Begin by stitching the top and bottom borders in tent stitch and then work the rest of the decorative areas, also in tent stitch, using the borders as your guide. Finish by working the background in basketweave.

VARIATIONS

If the footstool you are using is larger than the dimensions given here, you can increase the size of the pattern by inserting the same number of background-colored rows 20 rows from the top and bottom of the canvas.

FINISHING

The footstool base used for this project is a reproduction of one from the nineteenth century found in Hudson, New York. The turned legs and otherwise simple appearance are in perfect harmony with folk art. Because the needlepoint pattern is so intricate, adding brads or such seemed unnecessary, hence a simple welt that picked up the cornflower blue in the design.

✳ ✳ ✳

COLOR		PATERNAYAN	SKEINS
■	MOCHA BROWN	401	17
■	MEDIUM CORAL	842	4
▫	ECRU	262	2
◗	LIGHT GOLDEN BROWN	723	1
▢	TAN	497	2
◆	VERY DARK ANTIQUE BLUE	510	2
◉	LIGHT NAVY BLUE	502	2
○	VERY LIGHT ANTIQUE BLUE	514	1
~	VERY DARK GRAY GREEN	532	3
■	DARK TURQUOISE	533	2
◎	LIGHT TEAL	534	1

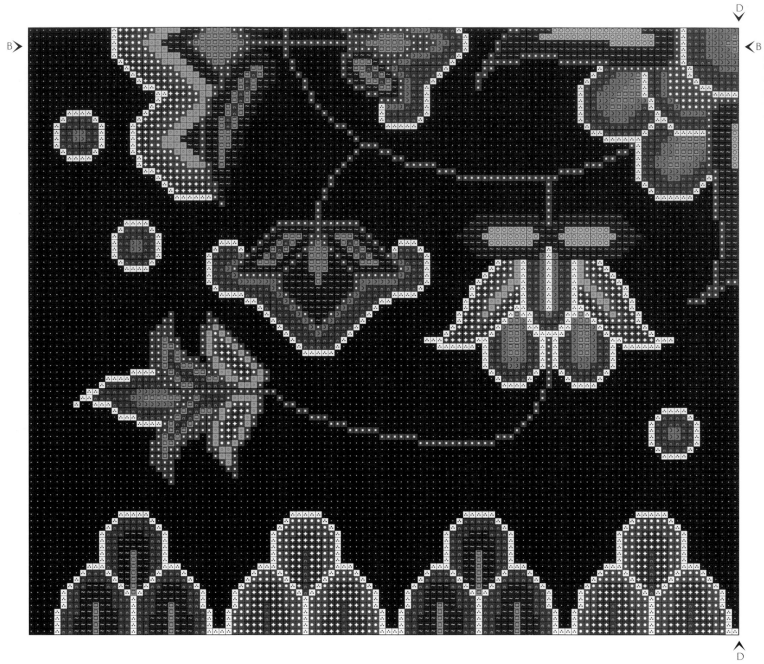

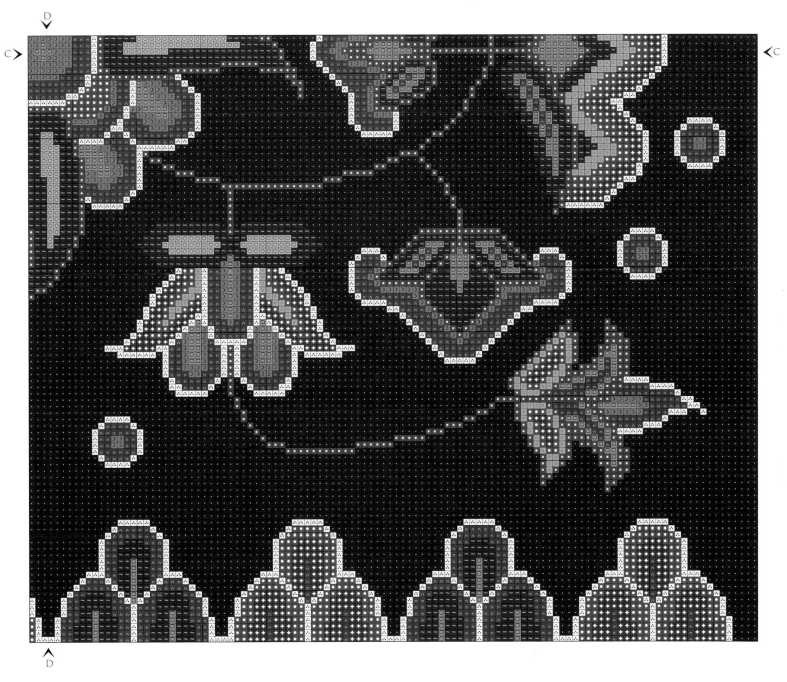

Pocketbook with Basket of Flowers

Artist unidentified

Pennsylvania, possibly Chester County; c. 1720–1750

Silk and metallic thread on silk over linen with spangles; 4½ x 5½" (11.5 x 14 cm) (closed)

Promised gift of Ralph Esmerian, P1.2001.292

FLORAL PURSE

"THERE IS NO BLUE WITHOUT YELLOW AND WITHOUT ORANGE."—*Vincent Van Gogh*

Blue skies, aquamarines, baby blue eyes, robin's eggs, swimming pool blue. . . . What is it about blue that we love? Blue is so popular that the makers of the Crayola crayon named their 100 billionth crayon Blue Ribbon. And for George Gershwin, his "Rhapsody in Blue" of 1924 was "a sort of musical kaleidoscope of America." Of all the colors, light blue connotes softness and tranquility, a deft touch of beauty. The blue grace notes here—the blue-and-tan silk dupioni purse, two-tone suede gloves by Geoffrey Beene, even the twilight-blue pearl ring—against the painted chest are just a little bit of true-blue heaven.

MATERIALS

canvas: 18-gauge mono canvas, 10 x 11" (25.5 x 28 cm)

thread: DMC Cotton Floss

needle: Size 22 tapestry

finished design: 6 x 7" (15 x 18 cm) (108 x 128 stitches)

stitches: Tent, Basketweave, Satin

skill level: Difficult

STITCHING

Use all six strands of the cotton floss. Stitch the decorative areas using tent stitch, and then use satin stitch for the flowers and leaves. Work the background in basketweave.

VARIATIONS

This pattern is for a single-sided purse. If you wish to needlepoint both sides, you can repeat the bottom portion of the pattern up to the row that separates the purse from the flap. You will need an additional piece of 10 x 10"

(25.5 x 25.5 cm) canvas and double the amounts of floss noted with an asterisk (★).

FINISHING

There are so many choices for completing this piece, but I decided on silk dupioni because the natural slubs complement the texture of needlepoint. Why the stripe? In part, to contrast with the overall floral design, and because it gave me two colors to enhance in the needlework design. Other details include a pale blue silk for the lining, an antique gold cord for the trim, and an upholstery tassel for the closure. If you prefer something dressy, you could use a velvet, in which case use a silk velvet because cotton velvet is too thick for this small purse. A vintage silk would look fantastic, and since you don't need much it wouldn't be expensive to pick up some at a flea market or vintage clothing shop.

COLOR		DMC FLOSS	SKEINS
⊡	VERY LIGHT TAN	739	5★
◕	LIGHT TAN	437	I
◘	VERY DARK DESERT SAND	632	I
✖	MEDIUM DESERT SAND	3773	I
∴	LIGHT TAWNY	951	I
▣	LIGHT COPPER	922	I★
✚	COPPER	921	I
◖	MEDIUM COPPER	920	3★
r	VERY DARK OLIVE GREEN	730	2★
⊠	LIGHT OLIVE GREEN	734	I★
◣	MEDIUM PARROT GREEN	906	I
0	LIGHT STRAW	3822	I★
▪	STRAW	3821	I★
⊘	DARK STRAW	3820	I★
▣	DELFT BLUE	828	I
◤	MEDIUM DELFT BLUE	799	I
✳	DARK DELFT BLUE	798	I

★*see variations*

A

·	739
◉	437
◨	632
✕	3773
∴	951
▫	922
+	921
⬭	920
┏	730
⊠	734
◗	906
0	3822
▪	3821
⊘	3820
▣	828
◤	799
✳	798

A

HEARTS

CHAPTER 4

❋

❋

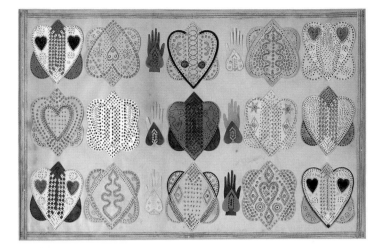

Heart-and-Hand Love Tokens

Artist unidentified

Probably New England; c. 1820

Watercolor and ink with gilt paper on cut and pinpricked

paper, mounted on paper; 9¼ x 14⅛" (23.5 x 36 cm)

Promised gift of Ralph Esmerian, P1.2001.256

DOUBLE HEART SCISSORS CASE

"BUT I WILL WEAR MY HEART UPON MY SLEEVE . . ."—*Shakespeare, from* Othello

The unintended bonus of doing needlepoint is all the extra thread you end up with after you finish a project, from Persian wool to silk floss and Pearl cotton. Having your own private stash makes it possible to create small projects using leftover colors, adding texture as you go along with miscellaneous threads such as metallic or variegated yarns. This scissors case is made with DMC Cotton Floss, which comes in a whopping 472 colors—now that's a lot of thread! The case sits on a pale pink commemorative porcelain ashtray with the inscription "H.M. King Edward VII Coronation 1937." The textured background is actually a New England pine writing box, c. 1840, with blue sponge decoration.

MATERIALS

canvas: 18-gauge mono canvas, 8 x 9" (20.5 x 23 cm)

thread: DMC Cotton Floss

needle: Size 22 tapestry

finished design: 3¹/₄ x 4" (8 x 10 cm) (59 x 74 stitches)

stitches: Tent, Basketweave, T-stitch

skill level: Moderate

STITCHING

Use all six strands of the cotton floss to work this project.
Begin with the smaller decorative areas using tent stitch,
and then work the larger areas of color in basketweave.
The background is worked in T-stitch.

VARIATIONS

This project can also be worked as a needle holder. Stitch
only the front; line the finished piece with a thin piece of
batting and cover with felt or other durable fabric. The
needles are then stuck into the felt, much like a pincushion.

FINISHING

There are many choices here, but I went the traditional
route and chose a little repeat that was a reproduction of
a nineteenth-century textile.

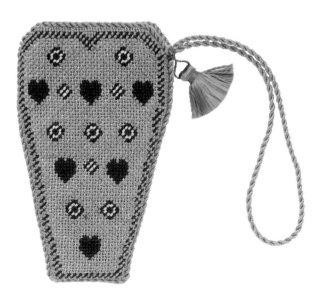

COLOR	DMC FLOSS	SKEINS
☒ CREAM	712	2
◨ VERY DARK BABY BLUE	803	1
⊡ LIGHT NAVY BLUE	312	1
⋈ VERY DARK SHELL PINK	221	1

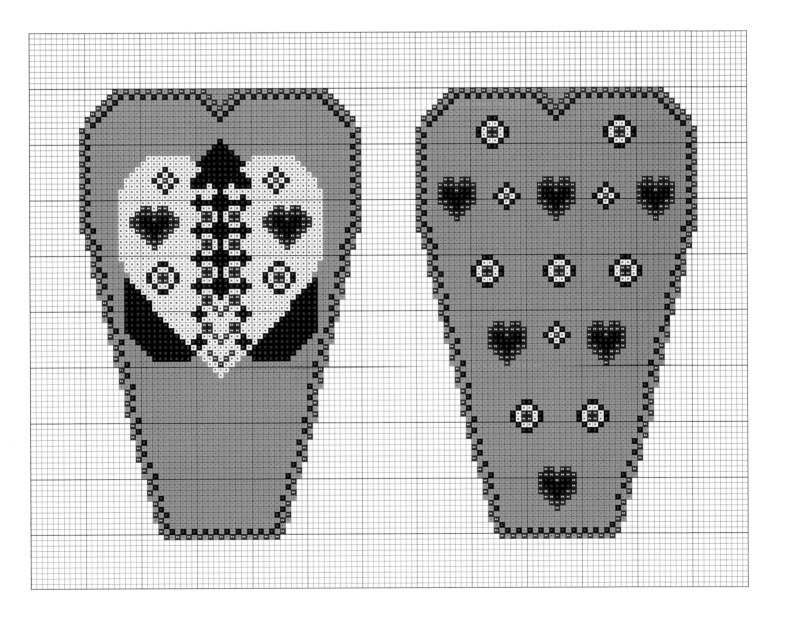

Pieties Quilt

Maria Cadman Hubbard (possibly 1769–?)

Probably Austerlitz, New York; 1848

Cotton; 88½ x 81" (225 x 206 cm)

Gift of Cyril Irwin Nelson in loving memory of his parents,

Cyril Arthur and Elise Macy Nelson, 1984.27.1

PIETIES BOLSTERS

"LITTLE ACTS OF KINDNESS, LITTLE WORDS OF LOVE / MAKE OUR EARTHLY EDEN LIKE OUR HEAVEN ABOVE"

This sprightly pair of bolsters, nestled in rather proper wing chairs, is a fitting anchor in this dining room, for their message would be an appropriate prayer before mealtime. Nearly a hundred years after these words, as part of an assortment of homilies, were first stitched on a quilt, Emily Post wrote that good manners are "the continuous practice of kind impulses." Who could argue the point, for shouldn't acts of kindness and love be part of daily life?

The folk art attributes here include the dazzling backdrop, an early twentieth-century Amish quilt with a pattern called "Sunshine and Shadow" from Lancaster County, Pennsylvania; a 1755 American Queen Anne tea table; and on it two pieces of porcelain—on the far right, an 1810 Chinese export porcelain cider jug, and in the center, an English oversized creamware pottery commemorative pitcher, c. 1800.

One last note: not all the sayings on the original quilt of 1848 were dour or religious. In particular consider the last one: "If you can / not be a / Golden pipp / in dont turn / crabapple."

MATERIALS

canvas: 12-gauge mono canvas, 21 x 11" (53.5 x 28 cm) for each piece

thread: DMC Pearl Cotton 3

needle: Size 20 tapestry

finished design: 16$\frac{1}{2}$ x 6$\frac{1}{4}$" (42 x 16 cm) (199 x 75 stitches) for each piece

stitches: Tent, Basketweave

skill level: Easy

STITCHING

Begin with stitching the border and then the letters, both in tent stitch (the border will serve as a guide for positioning the letters). Work the background in basketweave.

VARIATIONS

The yarn amounts given are for both sides of the cushion. If you only want one side—the front—you can halve the amount of yarn above. By the way, if red's not your thing, you can always do the lettering and border in a color more to your liking or room décor, again bearing in mind the more traditional folk art hues.

Because the Pieties Quilt has so many appealing sayings, we've included a chart for the complete alphabet should you want to adapt something other than the two we've provided.

FINISHING

The sayings on these bolsters were taken from a mid-nineteenth-century quilt stitched with various pious homilies, and we thought it would be fun to make two separate bolsters in which the sayings carried over, one to the other. In that case, putting them side by side on a bed seemed a natural, and I've since found they look good on matching chairs or as "bookends" on a couch. It would have been too easy to make the fabric exactly the same, so in this case I chose the same pattern but in two colorways, with contrasting welt.

COLOR		DMC PEARL	SKEINS
▪	VERY LIGHT BEIGE BROWN	543	10
◼	MEDIUM CHRISTMAS RED	304	8

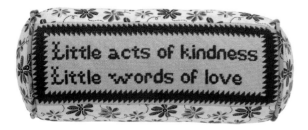

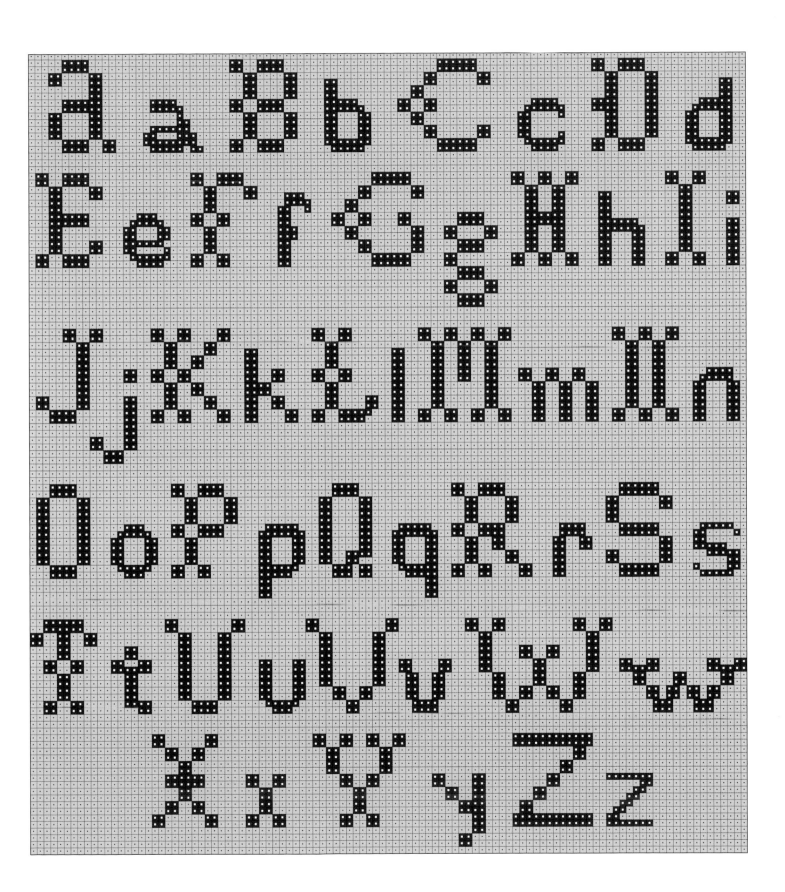

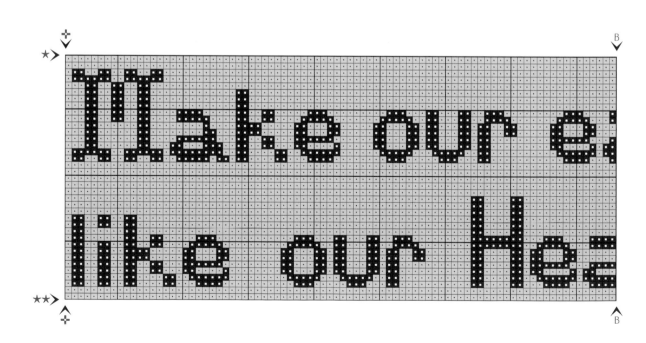

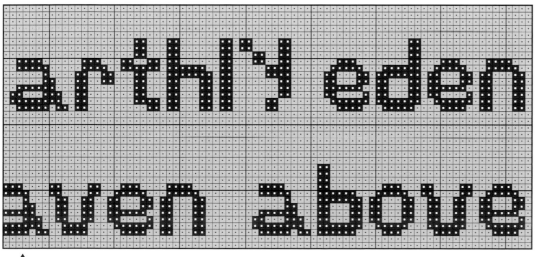

Box with Heart Decorations

George Robert Lawton (1813–1885)

Scituate, Rhode Island; c. 1842

Paint on pine, with leather hinges, lined with wallpaper and

newspaper remnants, printed engraving, and ink drawing;

10½ x 17½ x 12¾" (26.5 x 44.5 x 32.5 cm)

Promised gift of Ralph Esmerian, P1.2001.84

CHECKERBOARD-AND-HEARTS DOOR BRICK

✳ ✳ ✳

Other than a few words of caution, such as take care not to go barefoot and stub your toe, this is about the most becoming door stopper you could ever want in your home. It's bold, colorful, and were it not for the weight (it's not called a "door brick" for nothing), it's practically adorable. Although it's a fitting contrast on this painted black-and-white checkerboard floor, it would be just as attractive on wood, marble, or a carpet. As for the English springer spaniel, she's part of a collection of china figurines.

MATERIALS

canvas: 12-gauge mono canvas, 13 x 17" (33 x 43 cm)

thread: Paternayan wool

needle: Size 20 tapestry

finished design: 9 x 13" (23 x 33 cm) (158 x 108 stitches)

stitches: Tent, Basketweave

skill level: Difficult

STITCHING

To lessen the appearance of any show-through, use a brown or dark-colored canvas. Separate the strands of wool and only use two of the three strands to stitch the project. Begin with the decorative areas using tent stitch, and then work the larger areas of color in basketweave.

VARIATIONS

Why bother? This one is perfect, especially given how the little hearts line up along the sides. If you want to make the most minor of tweaks, you could swap out the coral for a deep green (think holly bushes) or a rich blue, such as Paternayan 550, either of which would go well with the dark brown-gray accents and the overall red-and-black color motif.

FINISHING

First and foremost, you need a brick. Construction sites are handy resources—there's always an extra brick or two lying around—or else you can get one from a building supply company. And while it may seem daunting to be your own bricklayer, so to speak, since you're handy with needlepoint, doing a little sewing isn't any harder. We used a black cotton canvas for the bottom of our brick, but you could use wool or even ultrasuede, provided your machine can accommodate the thicker fabric.

Making a brick cover is pretty much like making a pillowcase or any cushion cover. In theory, you prepare the three sides, insert the brick, close the end, and voilà—you have yourself a finished brick cover.

This pattern is designed to cover a standard-sized brick, measuring 8 x 4 x 2¼" (20.5 x 10 x 5.5 cm). For detailed instructions on making a brick cover, see page 141.

COLOR		PATERNAYAN	SKEINS
▼	ECRU	262	2
⌒	LIGHT CORAL	844	I
▣	BRICK RED	850	4
⊞	DARK BROWN GRAY	102	2
▪	BLACK	220	4

* * *

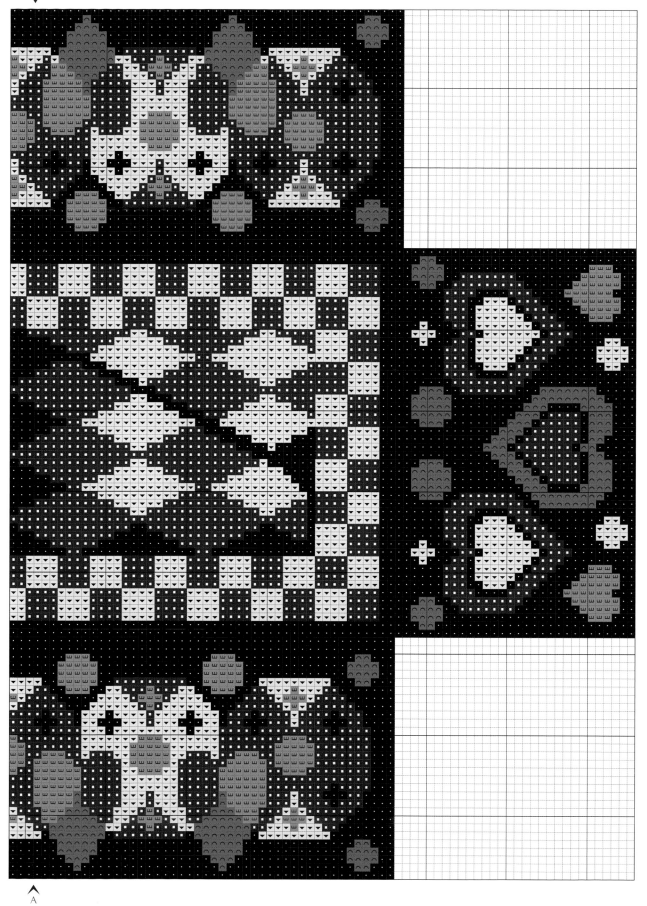

Heart-and-Hand Love Token

Artist unidentified

Possibly Connecticut; 1840–1860

Ink and varnish on cut paper; 12 x 14" (30.5 x 35.5 cm)

Museum purchase, 1981.12.15

LOVE TOKEN TOTE BAG

"HAND AND HEART SHALL NEVER PART / WHEN THIS YOU SEE / REMEMBER ME."

Well before Valentine's Day was commercialized by the greeting-card industry, wanting to give someone a genuine token of your affection dates back hundreds of years. Sweethearts in the eighteenth century would exchange paper love tokens—so-called because they could be given any day of the year that Cupid struck—in the shape of hands intertwined with hearts made with woven paper strips. That motif is employed here, with a total of twenty multicolored heart-in-hands on both sides of the bag. The result is a bit retro (it looks like something you might have found in your grandmother's closet) and thoroughly stylish. In this homeowner's kitchen, the cabinet above is filled with English Staffordshire Rabbitware pottery from around 1900.

MATERIALS

canvas: 12-gauge mono canvas, two pieces, each 17 x 22"
(43 x 56 cm)

thread: Paternayan wool

needle: Size 20 tapestry

finished design: Tote bag measuring 11 x 15½" (28 x 39.5
cm) (186 x 132 stitches) each side

stitches: Tent, Basketweave, Gobelin

skill level: Difficult

STITCHING

To lessen the appearance of any show-through, use a
brown or dark-colored canvas. Separate the wool and use
only two of the three strands to stitch the project. The yarn
amounts given will cover both pieces. Begin with the hands,
using both tent and basketweave stitches for the larger areas.
Work the background in basketweave. The border is a series
of blocks of gobelin stitch (follow the pattern for the direction
of the blocks of stitches) with four tent stitches in the middle.

VARIATIONS

The colors used here are a slight improvisation on the cut-
paper hearts and hands, known as love tokens, c. 1840–1860,
on which this was based. The easiest color to change is the
background, provided it doesn't fight with any of the colors
used for the hands. Bear in mind, however, that a light background color such as cream will quickly show dirt and wear.

If you're feeling ambitious and want to do a complete
overhaul of the colors, work out your selections on graph
paper with colored pencils to approximate the changes
you have in mind. A simpler variation would be something
monochromatic, such as a dark blue background with white
and red hands (so patriotic!), or shades of green.

FINISHING

This oversized bag has a slightly retro look and would look
stylish almost anywhere—even in a summer resort. For this
reason I went with square wood handles that emphasized the
quasi-vintage appeal of the tote. In New York's Garment
District there are many places to look for handles, but since
many shops now sell their goods online, you can easily avail
yourself of options beyond your local area. We used a sturdy
canvas for the lining, which seemed to me both practical
and traditional.

NOTE

The chart on pages 104–105 represents the side of the tote
as seen on page 100. The colors for the other side of the
tote, opposite, are indicated in the legend.

COLOR		PATERNAYAN	SKEINS
·	OLD GOLD	724	I HANK
I	CREAM	262	I
	BROWN	417	I
	ORANGE	842	I
	BLACK	220	I
	LIGHT YELLOW	734	2
	BURGUNDY	890	I
	LILAC	324	2
	YELLOW	815	2
	ROYAL BLUE	550	I
	GREEN	621	2
	RED	970	2
	BRICK RED	850	2

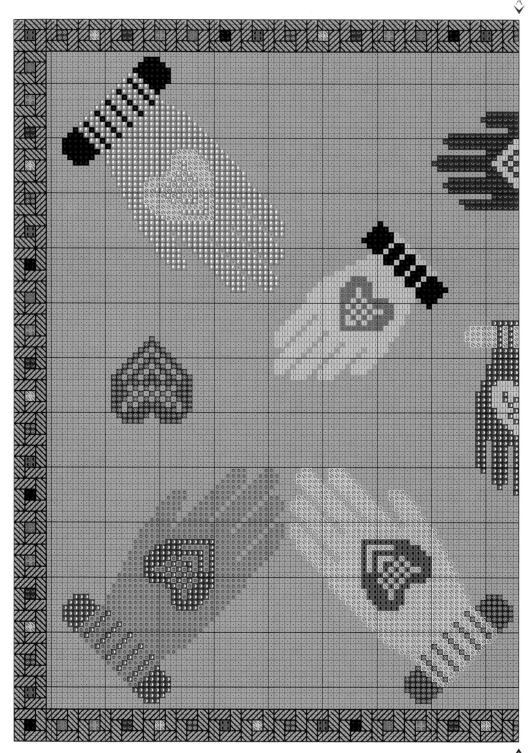

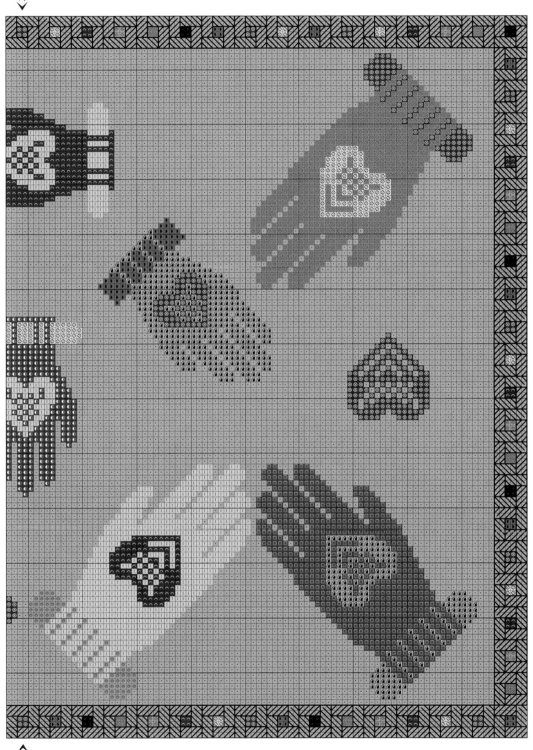

GEOMETRICS

CHAPTER 5

✳

✳

Chest of Drawers

Probably Johannes Mayer (1794–1883)

Mahantango or Schwaben Creek Valley, Pennsylvania; 1830

Paint on pine and poplar; $47\frac{1}{2}$ x $43\frac{3}{8}$ x 22"

(120.5 x 110 x 56 cm)

Museum purchase, 1981.12.3

COMPASS STAR
EYEGLASS CASE

❊ ❊ ❊

Just because hard cases are doled out with today's trendy designer sunglasses is no excuse not to have one made by loving hands—it's much more personal and appealing. So is a jaunty handkerchief.

MATERIALS

canvas: 14-gauge mono canvas, 8 x 12" (20.5 x 30.5 cm)

thread: DMC Cotton Floss

needle: Size 20 tapestry

finished design: 4 x 7½" (10 x 19 cm) (60 x 105 stitches)

stitches: Tent, Basketweave

skill level: Easy

STITCHING

Use all six strands of the cotton floss to work the pattern. For a more muted effect, stitch the pattern using two strands of Paternayan wool (see the conversion chart on page 142). Begin with the compass using the tent stitch, and then work the background and larger color areas in basketweave.

VARIATIONS

This is a project that is both quick and easy, given that the pattern is only for a needlepoint front. If you want to stitch both sides of the case, you will need an additional piece of 10 x 10" (25.5 x 25.5 cm) canvas. As for the design on the back, you can repeat the border, thus creating a checkerboard effect. Or you could repeat the compass star but revise the colors overall—the background could be black with the star in red, yellow, and green, with the border mirroring that done on the front. If you stitch the back, be sure to double the amount of floss.

FINISHING

It's only a little object, but I wanted to have some fun so I chose a houndstooth that had red, black, and green, lined the inside with an early American textile of thin black lines and tiny red dots, and then used a black cord for the piping. The result is an all-geometric case.

❊ ❊ ❊

COLOR		DMC FLOSS	SKEINS
⊙	MEDIUM YELLOW	743	I
◗	TANGERINE	742	I
▲	DARK CORAL	349	I
◖	VERY DARK CORAL	817	I
▪	FOREST GREEN	986	2
◉	BLACK	310	I

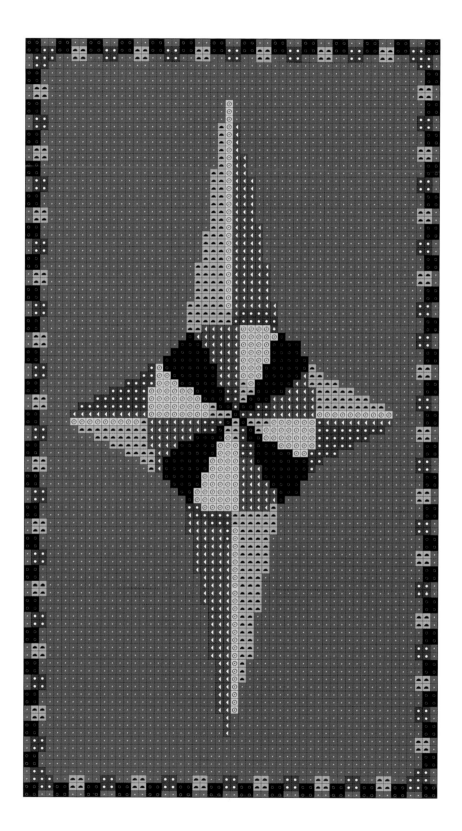

———— ⊚ ————

Log Cabin Quilt, Courthouse Steps Variation

Samuel Steinberger (1865–c. 1934)

New York; 1890–1910

Silk; 58 x 69¹/₂" (147.5 x 176.5 cm)

Gift of Cyril Irwin Nelson in honor of Robert Bishop, director (1977–1991),

American Folk Art Museum, 1990.17.8

———— ⊚ ————

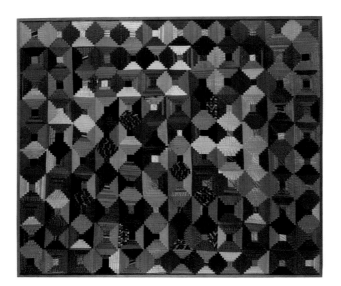

LOG CABIN MOTIF BELT

✴ ✴ ✴

There's a je ne sais quoi quality about miniature *anything* that never fails to charm, especially when it's a replica of something functional in our everyday lives. These four perfectly crafted chairs could have been made for dolls (what a lucky little girl to have owned these) or as samples to show the quality of a maker's work. Regardless, they are small gems. The pair at far left are mid-nineteenth-century American Federal New York or Baltimore miniature pine fancy side chairs; at center, with the hand-stitched belt, an American Baltimore classical revival miniature pine side chair, c. 1830; and at near right, a Pennsylvania pine and ash miniature rod back Windsor side chair with pink rose and green leaf motifs, also c. 1830. As they say, a change in perspective never hurts.

MATERIALS

canvas: 14-gauge mono canvas, 5" (12.5 cm) wide x desired length plus 5" (12.5 cm)

thread: DMC Cotton Floss

needle: Size 20 tapestry

finished design: 1¹/₂" (3.8 cm) wide; length varies according to waist size

stitches: Gobelin

skill level: Moderate

STITCHING

Use all six strands of floss for this project. The pattern shown is for a belt that is 26" (66 cm) long. Since this is a simple repeat, add as many diamonds as needed to extend the belt to the desired length. Each diamond is 1¹/₂" (3.8 cm) wide. The pattern is worked in a diagonal gobelin stitch.

VARIATIONS

The beauty of this pattern is that you can use any colors you like. It's also the perfect project for using up leftover thread. For the belt shown here, one skein of each color was used. If you want a simpler stitch, you can work this in tent stitch.

FINISHING

This is an easy project to personalize. Choose the sort of belt buckle you like as well as a leather color that works with your wardrobe. Although many needlepoint shops offer a selection of buckles, I bought my own, in this case a faux tortoiseshell. Certainly you can use a vintage buckle, perhaps even an old monogrammed one of your own.

COLOR	DMC FLOSS	SKEINS
± VERY LIGHT TAN	739	I
• LIGHT TAWNY	951	I
▲ MEDIUM DESERT SAND	3773	I
✚ DARK DESERT SAND	632	I
− MEDIUM YELLOW	743	I
◎ LIGHT TANGERINE	742	I
◖ TANGERINE	740	I
◣ COPPER	921	I
◗ CORAL	351	I
▶ ELECTRIC BLUE	996	I
V LIGHT NAVY BLUE	312	I
◖ DARK VIOLET BLUE	3746	I
⊗ DARK ANTIQUE VIOLET	3740	I
◿ LIGHT CRANBERRY	604	I
▪ CHRISTMAS RED	304	I
▪ BLACK	310	I

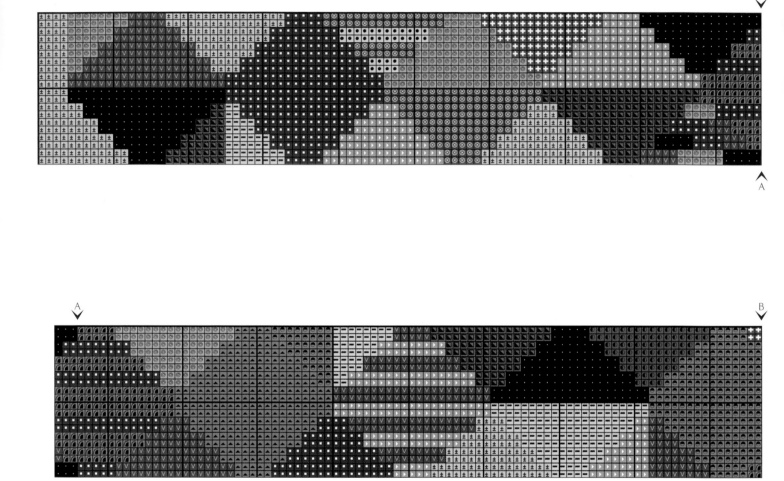

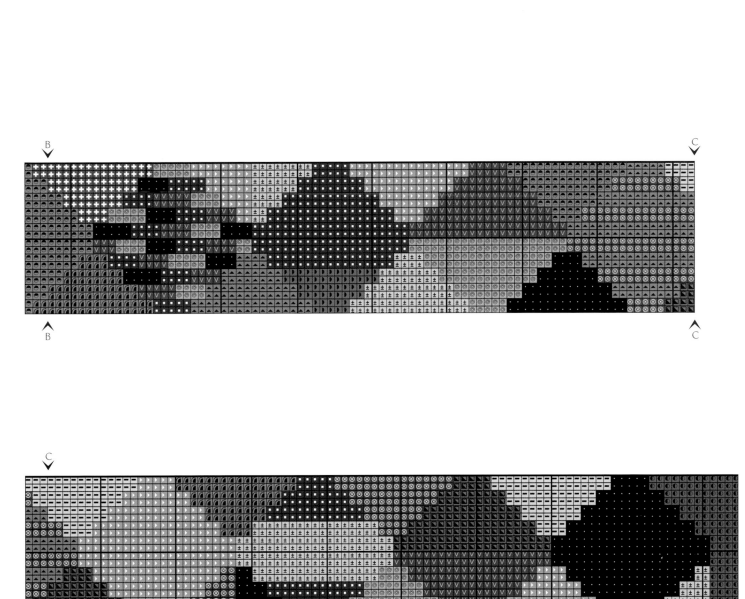

———— ⊚ ————

Tall Case Clock

Johannes Spitler (1774–1837)

Shenandoah County, Virginia; 1801

Paint on yellow pine, with brass and steel works, modern

watercolor and ink on period-paper face, and original

sheet-iron dial; 85½ x 14¾ x 8¼" (217 x 37.5 x 21 cm)

Gift of Ralph Esmerian, 2005.8.27

———— ⊚ ————

FRAKTUR-STYLE PICTURE FRAME

✳ ✳ ✳

The attributes of childhood: a favorite baseball collection and glove from the 1940s, a couple of sports trophies, a wood-carved spaniel, and above all, a framed family photograph of brothers and their sister.

MATERIALS

canvas: 14-gauge mono canvas, 21 x 23" (53.5 x 58.5 cm)

thread: DMC Pearl Cotton 3

needle: Size 20 tapestry

finished design: 16$\frac{1}{2}$ x 18$\frac{1}{2}$" (42 x 47 cm), to hold an 8 x 10" (20.5 x 25.5 cm) picture (240 x 265 stitches)

stitches: Tent, Basketweave, Satin

skill level: Moderate

STITCHING

To lessen the appearance of any show-through, use a brown or dark-colored canvas. Begin with the design elements using tent stitch, and then work the background in basketweave. For the navy blue diamonds, use satin stitch.

VARIATIONS

You can modify the emphasis on blue here simply by making the hearts or corner diamonds in the reddish terra cotta (221). If you do this, you will need an additional skein of terra cotta. You might want to consider making the moon either navy blue (823) or light blue (931).

FINISHING

This is physically such a large project that I kept the materials simple—a cotton canvas for the back and a simple gold cord to pick up on the border. Adding a piece of glass is optional, depending on the image you will be framing. If you want to adapt this frame by adding an easel back, keep in mind that it will need a fairly large surface for display.

I confess that my natural inclination is to have someone else do the finishing of this picture frame, but for more intrepid souls it's certainly a doable home project. If you can sew, you can make your own picture frame. Frankly, the materials needed aren't at all costly—masking tape, thick cardboard, heavy-duty scissors, and your fabric backing—making this a much thriftier project than giving it to your local framer.

It seems obvious to say, but before you get too invested in making this project, make sure that you have a photo that will perfectly fit the dimensions. Then again, even if you have to take just the "right" photo, it's worth it for this impressive needleworked frame.

For specific instructions on finishing the frame, see page 141.

COLOR	DMC PEARL	SKEINS
▲ ANTIQUE GOLD	729	3
○ LIGHT BLUE	931	1
· ANTIQUE BLUE	930	15
▣ NAVY BLUE	823	3
⬯ TERRA COTTA	221	3

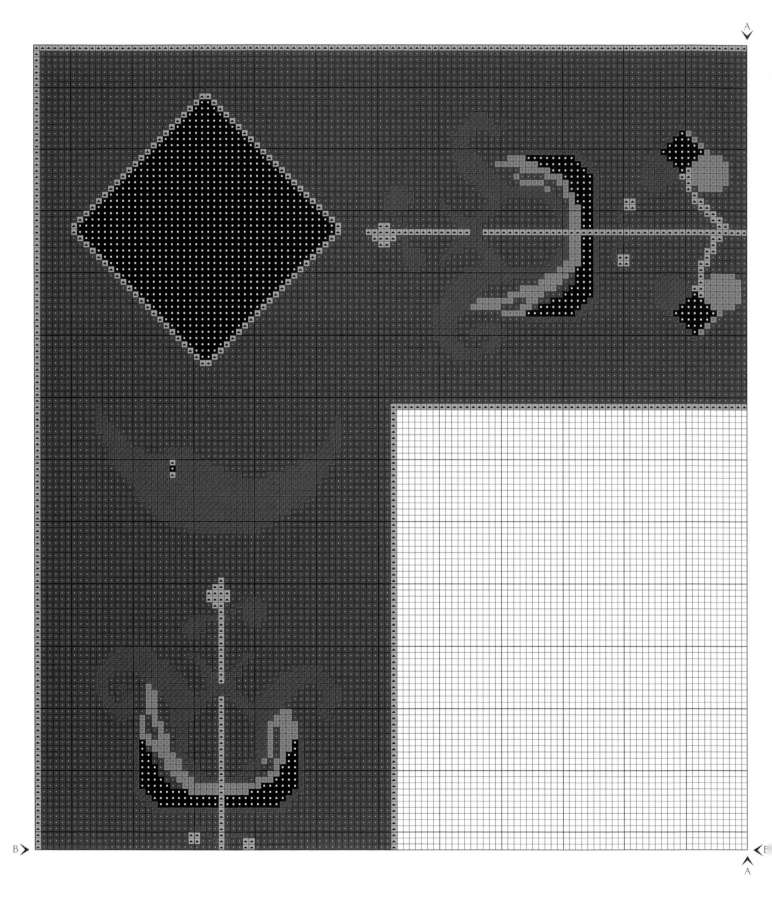

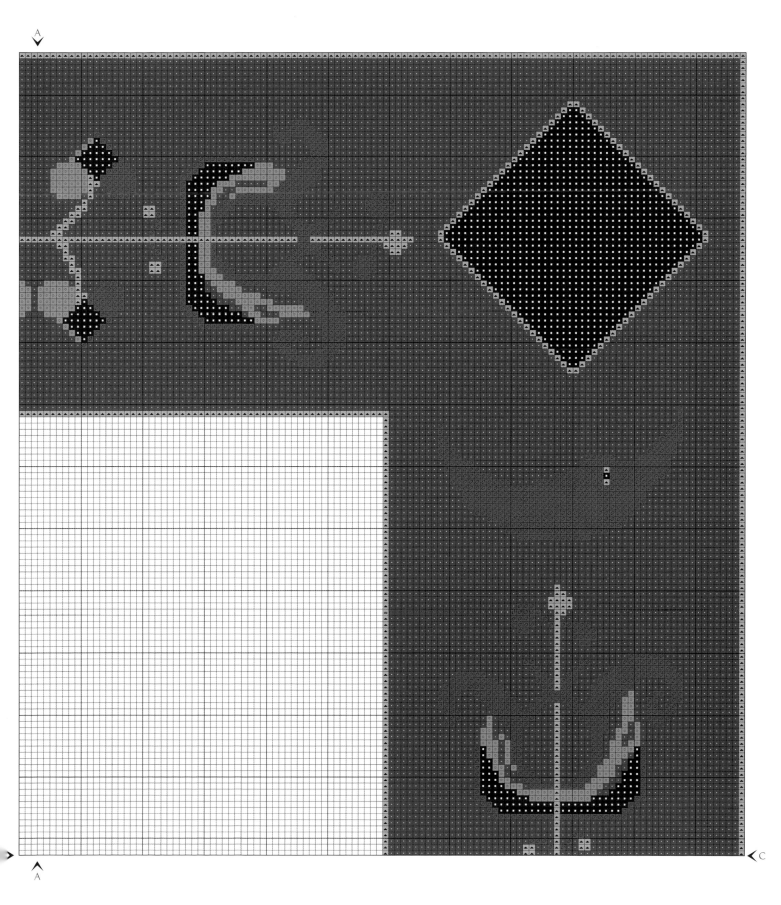

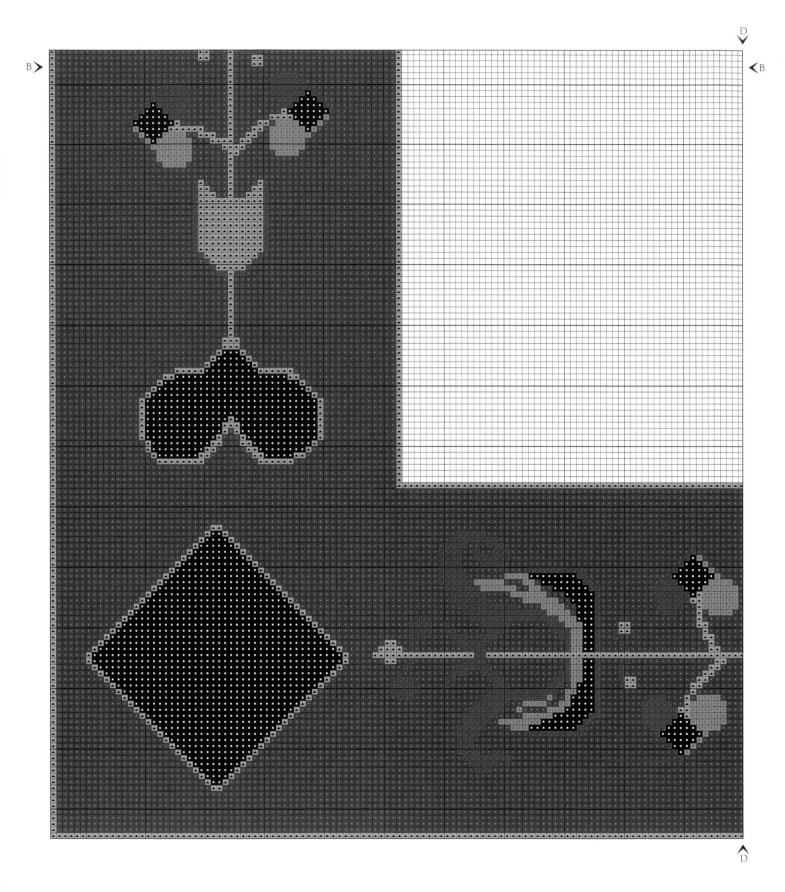

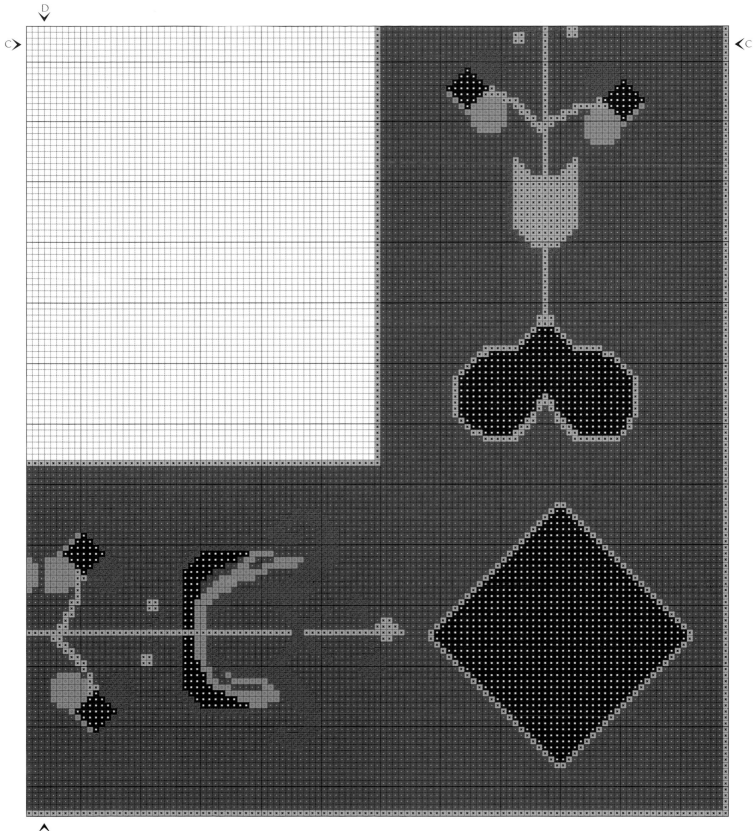

Round Box with Heart Decorations

George Robert Lawton (1813–1885)

Scituate, Rhode Island; c. 1840–1850

Paint on pine and maple; 2¼ x 7½" (5.5 x 19 cm) diameter

Promised gift of Ralph Esmerian, P1.2001.82

DARTBOARD
ROUND CUSHION

✳ ✳ ✳

The near-mesmerizing effect of the graphic cushion takes its inspiration from the top of a box whose radial-style design resembles both a compass and dartboard. The rich burgundy and navy hues of the couch absorb some of the "heat," as does the overall room décor. Just behind the couch is a painted wood mailbox, probably from Maine in the late 1800s, in the shape of a church; the chest at rear is actually a blanket chest covered in blue sponge paint. Net results: a bull's-eye!

MATERIALS

canvas: 14-gauge mono canvas, 19 x 19" (48.5 x 48.5 cm)

thread: Anchor wool

needle: Size 20 tapestry

finished design: 13" (33 cm) round (184 x 184 stitches)

stitches: Tent, Basketweave

skill level: Moderate

STITCHING

Begin by working the red outlines in tent stitch, followed by the dotted patterns. Use basketweave to fill in the larger areas of color.

VARIATIONS

Anchor wool on a 14-gauge canvas produces a very dense, tight weave. If you want a looser, more pliable weave, you can use a 12-gauge mono canvas, which would result in a 15$\frac{1}{4}$" (38.5 cm) finished piece.

FINISHING

This reminds me of a dartboard, so I made it even more vibrant by adding the blue-and-white oversized cord but kept the fabric rich and clean with a dark navy velvet. By the way, make sure the project is finished as a boxed pillow or else it will end up looking like a big wobbly orb.

❋ ❋ ❋

COLOR		ANCHOR	SKEINS
⊡	CREAM	8006	3
◸	YELLOW	8138	7
◀	RED	8442	8
▬	LIGHT BLUE	8792	6
◪	DARK BLUE	8638	6

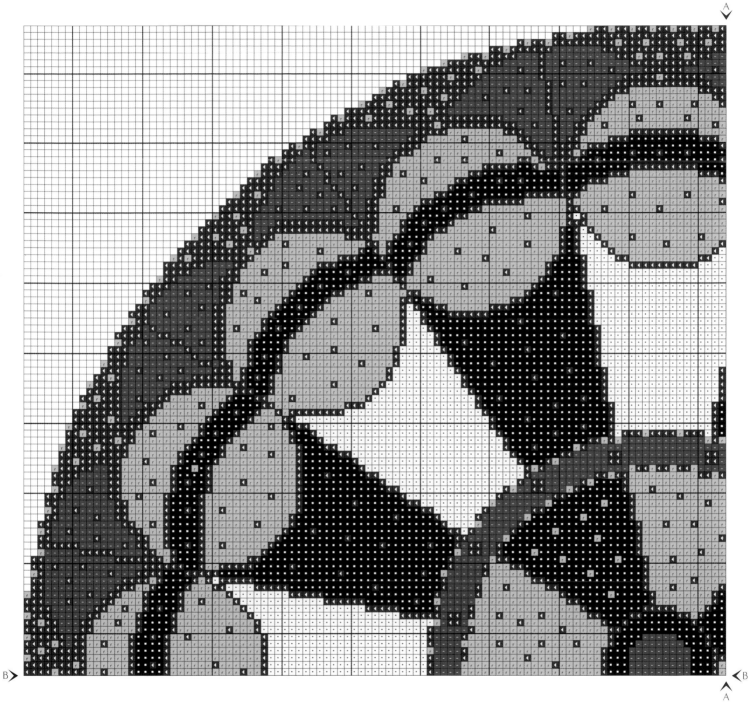

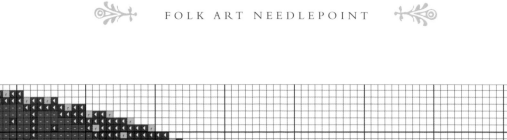

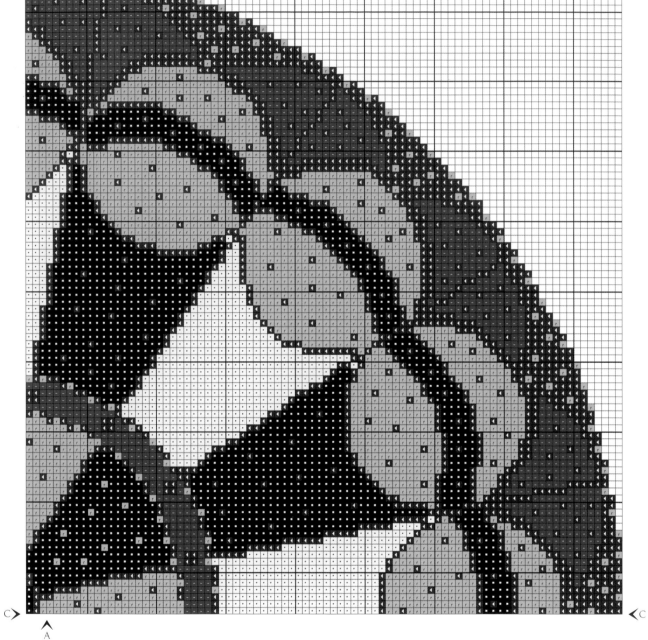

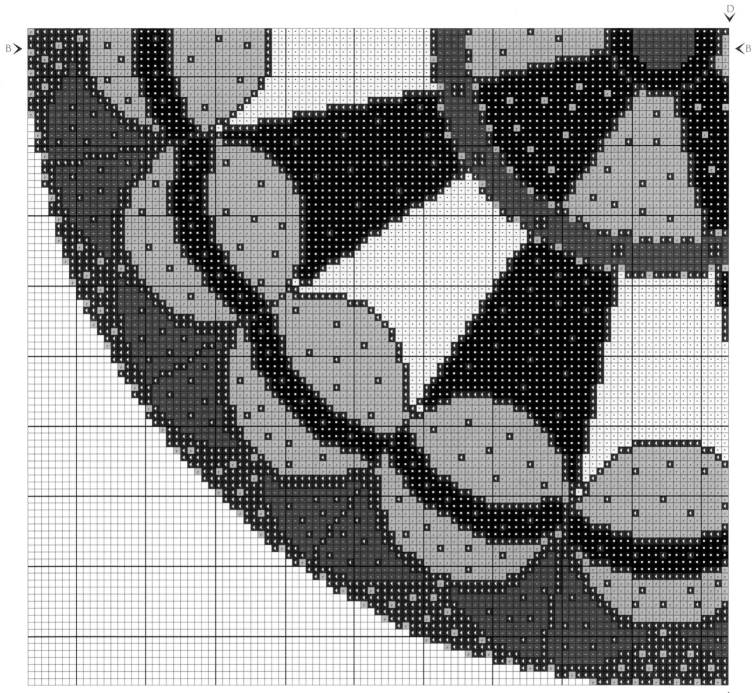

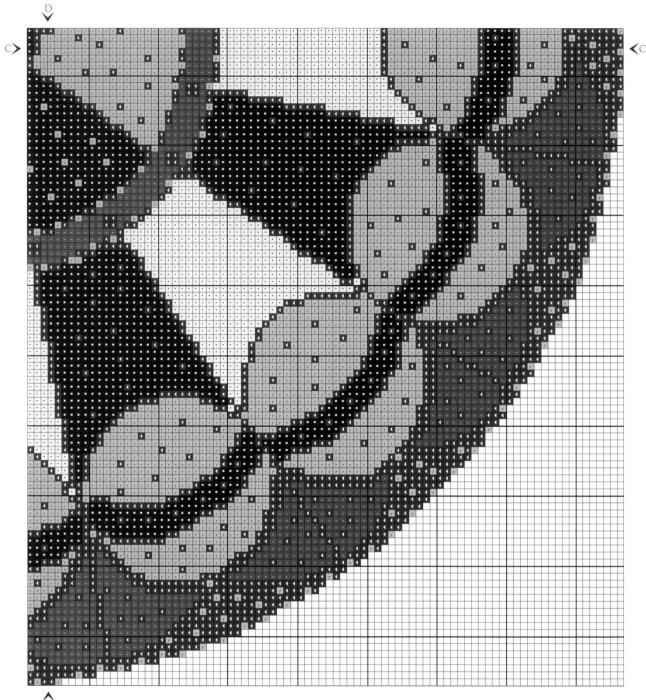

AMERICAN FOLK ART MUSEUM COMMENTARIES ON THE PLATES

❋ ❋ ❋

DAILY LIFE

Reiter Family Album Quilt

————— ◦ —————

Mourning quilts traditionally are created to memorialize a loved one and to help survivors cope with their pain. Such was the motivation for the making of this album quilt. Katie Friedman Reiter and her mother, Liebe Gross Friedman, each lost a child within a short period of time. Both were born in Slovakia and lived through economic depression and rampant anti-Semitism in eastern Europe. In 1885, Liebe sent twelve-year-old Katie to America in the belief that the New World would offer greater opportunities for a better life. In 1890, after living for five years with relatives in Newark, New Jersey, Katie married and moved to the steel town of McKeesport, Pennsylvania. Reasonably comfortable financially, Katie was able to send for her mother, her sister, Amelia, and her brother, Ephraim, in 1891. Katie's infant son, Adolph, died later that year, and Ephraim drowned in the Youghiogheny River shortly thereafter.

The Reiter quilt bears a strong resemblance to the album appliqué quilts that became popular in Germanic communities in Pennsylvania, New Jersey, and New York in the mid-nineteenth century. Although Orthodox Jews, the Reiters were assimilated into the McKeesport community and had access to fairs where quilts were shown and related periodicals and guides were offered. Katie may also have been exposed to the bold and brightly colored album quilts made in the vicinity of Newark, which also featured a strong German enclave. The *Reiter Family Album Quilt*, comprising sixteen embellished pictorial quilt blocks and bordered by blocks that form an overall design of undulating vines interspersed with floral sprays, relates closely to a quilt (c. 1850) possibly made by Mrs. Josiah Goodman in the collection of the Maryland Historical Society, Baltimore. The American eagle,

heavily symbolic to immigrant families, is placed prominently in one square. Two equestrian figures in black are thought to represent the two deceased children—*Reiter* means "rider" in German.

Katie cut apart the quilt in 1933 and fashioned from the pieces a crib quilt for her granddaughter, Leba Katherine, the firstborn of her youngest child, Theresa. In 1976, after the death of her husband, Leba Katherine Wine took a quiltmaking class and invited her mother to collaborate on a quilt. Her mother gently refused but encouraged Leba to reassemble the family quilt. She had it restitched professionally and during the process uncovered many family memories among her relatives. She also went on to create several of her own quilts, continuing the quiltmaking tradition in the Reiter family.

—Lee Kogan

Mary H. Huntington

————— ◦ —————

By the time this miniature was painted, portraits "in lyttle" had a well-established foothold in America. Drawing upon European limning traditions that had evolved from illuminated manuscripts, portrait miniatures were most frequently painted in a water-based medium on vellum, card, or ivory and housed in a small box or locket. Sometimes, miniature portraits were painted from full-scale ones and, conversely, served as prototypes for large portraits. The private act of viewing a miniature, nestled in the palm of a hand or in a locket worn around the neck, was in direct opposition to the public sense of full-size portraiture.

This enchanting miniature depicts Mary Hallam Huntington (1813–1820) at the age of about one year. The tiny handmade pasteboard box, covered with a single motif from an embossed wallpaper, protects the precious miniature from harm and provides an element of surprise when it is opened to reveal the delicate child. Little Mary stands in profile, one foot forward, wearing a cream-colored gown with a sheer overdress and bonnet

of fine white netting. A smudge of green provides a horizontal floor plane, and a shadow delineates her pale dress and profile against the light-colored background. She wears a blue slipper on one foot and holds the other slipper in her hand—a pose that has been used as an effective compositional device in depictions of young children by artists including John Brewster Jr. It has been conjectured that in some cases, the "one shoe off" motif indicates a postmortem portrait. Mary Huntington, however, died in 1820, before her seventh birthday but well after the date this portrait was painted.

—Stacy C. Hollander

Close Finish Hooked Rug

————— ◦ —————

The "New England Kitchen" display at the Philadelphia Centennial Exposition of 1876 sparked an interest in America's colonial heritage that presaged the Colonial Revival movement. For many women, this translated into a renewed regard for simple materials and good handcraftsmanship applied to ordinary household items, and no fashionable Colonial Revival interior was complete without a spinning wheel in the corner, a cotton quilt on the bed, and a hooked rug on the floor. The exposition also included a display of English bicycles that sparked a cycling craze in America through the end of the century. From 1890 until 1896, the number of cyclists rose from about 150,000 to 4 million. The fad inspired the institution of professional cycling clubs and bicycle races, which became increasingly popular during the 1890s. After this period, widespread interest in cycling diminished, replaced by automobile driving and other activities. The imagery on this rug suggests a date between the 1880s and 1890s, when the high-wheelers depicted in the scene were in their heyday. It is more likely, however, that it was made during the Colonial Revival period, when hooked rugs began to exhibit a taste for nostalgic scenes with related texts.

—Stacy C. Hollander

Situation of America, 1848.

Early landscapes and architectural depictions were usually painted on interior architectural elements such as overmantels and fire boards. These forms provided an ornamental focus to the fireplace, one of the most important features of early American homes. Overmantels typically were painted directly on plaster or wood paneling that covered the chimney, but they occasionally appeared on canvas. This late example continues the tradition of architectural depictions on overmantels and draws its inspiration from engraved and published town views that had become popular by this time. It shows the New York City skyline of closely clustered buildings as viewed from Brooklyn, across the East River. Billows of smoke issue from the paddle-wheeler *Sun* (built in 1836 with New York as its home port) and the freight train on the wharf, emphasizing the strong ties between economic growth—which had been spurred by shipping on the Erie Canal and overland rail transport—and architectural development. The dome of City Hall appears disproportionately large behind the prominent warehouse situated on the Brooklyn dock. According to an earlier published source, *Situation of America, 1848.* was removed from the Squire Phillips home in Brookhaven, Long Island, New York, but this home has not been identified and the information has not been documented.

—Stacy C. Hollander

Horse and Rider Weathervane

This rare cast-iron weathervane, which surmounted a barn in Francistown, New Hampshire, for a hundred years or so, highlights the diversity of weathervanes made in the nineteenth century. Perched on a galloping horse, an acrobatic figure holds an oversize arrow as if it were a spear he is about to hurl. The top of the figure's head and left hand are flared to accept two screws that fix the arrow to them, indicating that this is the weathervane's original configuration. A photograph of the weathervane while it was still installed on the barn shows the arrow in this position, not in the more customary location below the horse.

The profile of the horse is reminiscent of some copper weathervanes attributed to A. L. Jewell of Waltham, Massachusetts. This is not to suggest that it was made by Jewell but to underscore the influence of his designs on other makers. Cast iron may seem to be an unlikely material for weathervanes, given their need to turn freely in the wind. Then again, their symbolic and decorative functions have always been just as important, and, by the second half of the nineteenth century, other methods of indicating wind direction were available. Two other types of cast-iron weathervanes are known. An unidentified workshop that probably operated in New Hampshire or Maine around mid-century produced a distinctive style of horse, also known today as a "formal horse," and a rooster, both of which have cast-iron bodies and sheet-iron tails.

—Ralph Sessions

BIRDS, BEASTS & BUGS

Appliquéd Carpet

It is thought that this extraordinary room-size appliquéd and embroidered textile is a floor cover, but its pristine condition belies its use in this function. Because of its complex design and masterful execution, it has been likened to the *Embroidered Carpet* made by Zeruah Higley Guernsey Caswell in Castleton, Vermont, now in the collection of the Metropolitan Museum of Art, New York. But it is also related to a small number of appliquéd floor and bed coverings made in Maine from about 1845 until about 1870. These textiles are characterized by whimsical pictorial elements in a block set surrounded by a border. This example is further elaborated by a central medallion with a tapestry-inspired scene of two trees, with birds in the branches, tall grasses, and a blue rabbit. Two opposing inside corners are further distinguished by dense branching appliqués, and a wreathlike motif is centered on four sides. Rather than the rigid square or rectangular block seen in the other examples, the repeated flower motifs are separated by arch-shaped leafy branches, lending a dynamism to the conventionalized overall pattern.

Appliqué gained favor as a technique for small table and hearth rugs about 1840. As in quiltmaking, the appliqué technique involves cutting elements from one fabric and stitching them onto a different fabric foundation. Early designs often feature an urn with sprawling flowers, but the pieces from Maine show a particular sense of freedom in their compositions. Because the shapes are cut out rather than pieced, there is great pictorial flexibility, evident in this monumental textile.

—Stacy C. Hollander

Hannah Carter Canvaswork Picture

Hannah Carter's elegant lady in a pastoral setting belongs to colonial Boston's most famous form of needlework, featuring the so-called fishing lady motif. It first captured the attention of collectors and scholars when seven canvaswork pictures featuring an identical lady holding a fishing pole were published in 1923. It was 1941, however, before convincing evidence was offered that these and related pastoral embroideries were worked by young girls who were attending Boston boarding schools. Twelve fishing ladies were recorded within a group of fifty-eight related pieces, and eventually they all became known as "fishing lady" pictures, with or without the pole or the lady. Today, seventeen pieces that depict the fishing lady are known, but only six makers have been identified, and the schools they attended have defied discovery. The close similarity of motifs in Hannah's embroidery, especially the flowering tree at left, leaves little doubt that she was taught by the fishing lady instructress.

The artist's identity may never be proven, but the most likely Hannah Carter was born in Boston on August 31, 1732. She was the eldest child of shipwright Ralph Carter (1700–?) and Sarah Bomer Thompson (1705–?), who were married by Dr. Joseph Sewall at the Old South Church on November 21, 1731. She may also have been the Hannah Carter who married rope maker Thomas Ayres (1728–?) on July 12, 1753.

—Betty Ring

Bird of Paradise Quilt Top

Some of the most decorative American quilts are those appliquéd with motifs cut from one fabric and stitched to another. Motifs for the earliest appliqué quilts were cut from block-printed chintzes and applied to another fabric to form new designs, a technique that has been called *broderie perse* or "cut-out chintz appliqué." The appliqués in the *Bird of Paradise Quilt Top* include a doll-like girl, paired animals, famous racehorses of the day, and the bird with extravagant tail feathers after which the quilt top is named.

The appliquéd elements were made using templates cut from newsprint that descended with the bedcover. The collection of patterns includes the figure of a man who does not appear on the block next to the woman on the quilt top, suggesting that the bedcover may have been made in anticipation of a wedding. Because the papers used in the templates date from between 1858 and 1863—encompassing the Civil War years—it has been speculated that the wedding never took place, and for that reason the top was never quilted and completed.

—Stacy C. Hollander

FLOWERS

Cross River Album Quilt

Album quilts of the mid-nineteenth century grew out of a fondness for autograph albums, a trend that is believed to predate the fabric examples in this quilt by approximately twenty years. By the 1840s, women were signing quilt blocks and sewing them together for a variety of reasons: to raise money for a charitable cause, to celebrate a particular event, to honor a distinguished member of the community, as a gift for a departing

family member or friend, or simply as an expression of friendship and community. As yet, the exact purpose for the making of the *Cross River Album Quilt* has not been determined; however, all the eleven women who signed the quilt in 1861 have been located in historical records. All were probably related and lived within a mile or two of each other. They were of average means and ranged in age from fifteen to fifty-five.

There may have been a patriotic reason for making this quilt, which is dated "November 1st 1861" in the square signed by Eldad Miller. The year 1861 marked the start of the Civil War, and the Soldiers Aid Society was active in the area raising funds through private contributions, fairs, and entertainments. At the bottom center of the quilt is a block in a flag design that has been enhanced with the embroidered word *Union* and appliquéd stars. In June 1861, shortly before this quilt was dated, *Peterson's Magazine* printed a colored illustration for a red, white, and blue quilt in a very similar design under the caption "A Patriotic Quilt." The magazine was trying to inspire readers to quilt their Union sympathies, and this block points at least to patriotic feelings among the makers if not to a war-related purpose behind the construction of the bedcover.

—Elizabeth V. Warren

Centennial Quilt

Bedcovers decorated primarily by the conventional appliqué technique (as opposed to the cut-out chintz method) became popular among American quiltmakers in the early 1840s. In this type of decoration, the quiltmaker cuts her own designs, either freehand or with a pattern, rather than one already printed on fabric. This change in the look of American quilts often is attributed to the adoption of quiltmaking by Pennsylvania Germans beginning in the 1830s.

A variety of popular Germanic motifs decorate this pieced and appliquéd bedcover: the facing birds, tulips, lilies, hearts, baskets, leaves, stars, and rosettes are all designs found on a wide array of Pennsylvania German folk art forms. Many of the images have been interpreted to have symbolic meaning. The lily and the

tulip, for example, have been called symbols of purity and of the Virgin, as well as attributes of the archangel Gabriel. Whether or not this quilt had religious meaning to its maker, a G. Knappenberger, she made it clear that it was created in honor of the nation's centennial celebration in 1876 by adding the word *centennial* and the date *1876* to her design. From visual evidence, the quilt has been assigned to Pennsylvania, not far from the site of the Centennial Exposition in Philadelphia. The G. Knappenberger whose name appears on this quilt has not been identified, but a descendant of a woman named Gertrude Knappenberger saw a photograph of the quilt and informed the museum that the quiltmaker was likely her great-great-grandmother. According to family information, Knappenberger lived in Emmaus, Pennsylvania, and would have been between sixty and seventy years old in 1876.

—Elizabeth V. Warren

Packard Bed Rug

This is one of at least three bed rugs produced by members of the Packard family of Jericho, Vermont. Dated within one year of each other, the two textiles share a basic geometric layout, though there is some variance in individual floral and geometric motifs. Bed rugs were made from the early eighteenth century through the early decades of the nineteenth. Originally it was believed that they were particular to the Connecticut River Valley, but it has since been established that they were made throughout New England. Although bed rugs resemble later hooked rugs, they were worked with a needle and usually were yarn sewn in a running stitch through a foundation of wool or sometimes linen. Small loops left on the surface could be clipped to form a pile or left unclipped, as in this example, giving a flat, chenille-like appearance. These large and heavy bedcovers represented an impressive investment of time and effort. Makers usually gathered raw materials specifically for the project, and because bed rugs were almost invariably home produced, this meant raising the sheep that provided the wool, which then needed to be spun and dyed. Designs were carefully conceived to ensure that enough material to produce a pattern was made all at once.

The design of this bed rug is reminiscent of strapwork, an ornamental scrollwork often seen in Mannerist decoration, and this connection further demonstrates the endurance of aesthetic ideas introduced into New England more than a century before. The flat pile and geometric layout with separate floral and clamshell elements also show the influence of Transylvanian-type rugs with strapwork designs that are displayed on tables in some colonial portraits. Turkeywork rugs, with similar designs, were imported directly into the American colonies from Europe. There, authentic Turkish rugs had influenced northern European craftsmen, particularly in the textile centers in the Netherlands. During the seventeenth century, when some of these craftsmen immigrated to America, their ideas were absorbed into various decorative arts and were also received by women who incorporated them into their home-produced textiles.

—Stacy C. Hollander

Pocketbook with Basket of Flowers

In 1597, John Gerard (1545–1612) published *The Herball or Generall Historie of Plantes*, whose illustrations became a primary source for needlework patterns. The basket of flowers stitched on this tiny pocketbook appears to take its cue from one such illustration; the diamond patterning on Gerard's basket and the cross-hatching of a pineconelike flower are loosely interpreted in needlework stitches. English embroidery traditions greatly influenced American needlework, especially in urban areas, where professional needleworkers advertised their services. Levy Simons, probably once a member of the English Embroiderer's Guild in London, advertised himself in the *New York Mercury* of October 9, 1758, as an "Embroiderer from LONDON," and that he "worked in Gold or Silver, shading in Silk or Worsted."

The flowers worked in crewel on this small pocketbook are shaded in silk. The technique, as described in Simons's advertisement, was used to spectacular effect in large-scale projects such as bed furnishings but is less common in this small format.

Metallic threads and spangles continued to be used in pictorial needleworks of the late eighteenth and early nineteenth centuries, when popular taste dictated neoclassical forms and shimmery silk-on-silk embroideries, with the effect heightened by the use of reflective materials such as spangles and mica flakes.

—Stacy C. Hollander

HEARTS

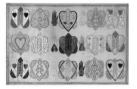

Heart-and-Hand Love Tokens

———— ⊚ ————

Love tokens, often mistakenly called valentines, were given in affection on days other than February 14. In this exuberant example, fifteen hearts and six heart-and-hand motifs are applied in horizontal rows to a sheet of paper. Most of the twenty-one elements use pin work to create a lacy effect, as well as woven strips of paper in an interlacing technique suggestive of love never ending. The heart-and-hand is generally associated with love or friendship and probably originated from Valentine's Day customs. In one tradition, a man gave a woman the gift of a glove, which she then wore in acceptance of his proffered love. In another, a woman gave a man her glove, which he then wore pinned to his sleeve for the duration of the day. The well-known phrase "wearing your heart on your sleeve" derives from this custom.

—Stacy C. Hollander

Pieties Quilt

———— ⊚ ————

Religious devotion motivated Maria Cadman Hubbard to make the *Pieties Quilt*, in which pious homilies in red letters are set within the blocks and half blocks of a diamond grid with diagonal sawtooth sashing. Also featured are religious and secular sayings in sixteen blocks with red letters, among them "Little acts of kindness / Little words of love," "Make our earthly

eden / like our Heaven above," "abide / with / us," "Love one / another," "thy will / be done," "Is our / Home a / Heaven," "Heaven / is our / Home," and "If you can / not be a / Golden pipp / in dont turn / crabapple."

The inscription "Maria / Cadman / Hubbard / aged 79" appears in a square near the bottom left, and the date "1848" appears on the bottom right. The sawtooth border, sashing, and pattern around the geometric forms give the design a feathered look. Several New York State quilts with similarly pieced lettering suggest the existence of a regional style. The identity of the quiltmaker remains something of a mystery. She may have been Maria Cadman Hubbard of Austerlitz, New York, a daughter of William Cadman of Mt. Pleasant and granddaughter of John and Phebe Cadman, who later became Mrs. Maria Hubbard of Troy, New York.

—Lee Kogan

Box with Heart Decorations

———— ⊚ ————

This exuberantly decorated box is one of a few originally believed to have been made by John Colvin, a Rhode Island woodworker, builder, and carpenter. They have since been established as the work of another Rhode Island craftsman, George Robert Lawton, whose family was related to Colvin's by marriage. Lawton was born in Newport, the son of Robert Lawton and Sarah Anthony. He married Rosinda Searle (1816–1885) in Scituate, Rhode Island, where they raised their five children. At least sixteen pieces that can be attributed to Lawton descended in the family.

Although the flurry of hearts on this box might seem to suggest a Pennsylvania German influence, Lawton was of English heritage, with deep roots in Rhode Island. The proliferation of hearts, checkerboards, and other geometric motifs are incised into the wood and painted. The box is lined with newspapers that bear the date 1842, giving an indication of the period during which Lawton worked. It is of simple construction, with rabbeted and nailed corners and leather hinges. The box is, however, outstanding for its complex painted decoration, carefully planned and executed.

—Stacy C. Hollander

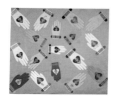

Heart-and-Hand Love Token

Valentine's Day is generally considered the first annual occasion on which greetings in the form of tokens and keepsakes were exchanged. The custom of giving presents, gloves in particular, to one's sweetheart is noted as early as the seventeenth century: "I resolved him as the other company did; which afterwards giving gloves unto their Valentines, wee also bought a paire costing 2s.6d. and bestowed them upon her" (William Waldegrave, May 18, 1608). In his famous diary (written 1660–1669), Samuel Pepys also cites Valentine gift-giving, and by the eighteenth century, sweethearts cut love tokens of paper in the shape of hands intertwined with separate hearts with woven paper strips. Such expressions of affection became so popular that during the mid-nineteenth century, publications such as *Godey's Lady's Book* and *Harper's Weekly* were suggesting Valentine's Day verses and cut-paper projects for both men and women.

Cut-paper hearts and hands are more correctly termed "love tokens" because they were given as gestures of regard on days other than Valentine's Day. This love token is an assemblage of seventeen paper hands with a paper heart interwoven on each palm; a contrasting strip of paper is woven through the wrists. The hearts are different sizes—some are varnished, and two incorporate pieces of ruled paper. One hand carries the familiar sentiment "Hand and heart shall never part / When this you see / Remember me."

—Stacy C. Hollander

GEOMETRICS

Chest of Drawers

Immigrants of Germanic heritage started coming to America during the seventeenth century, attracted by William Penn's invitation to establish communities in the fertile lands of Pennsylvania. The Pennsylvania Germans have long been celebrated for the richness of the culture they brought and maintained for generations, but within their embracing culture, self-contained pockets of settlement produced distinctive traditions. The Mahantango Valley, bounded by Line Mountain on the north and Mahantango Mountain on the south, was settled in the eighteenth century, primarily by second-generation Germans from other southeastern Pennsylvania communities. A tradition of decorated furniture specific to this region had developed by the turn of the nineteenth century.

It is thought that one of the major contributors to this group of furniture was Johannes Mayer, whose home, which still stands in Upper Mahanoy Township, was discovered to contain moldings and trims identical to those used in fifty-seven chests of drawers, slant-front desks, cupboards, and hanging cupboards made between 1827 and 1841. The painted embellishments include motifs typical of Pennsylvania German decorative arts: tulips, birds, animals, and other flowers. But the cartouche-shaped reserves on the drawer fronts outlined in delicate striping and the quarter-fans in the corners are ornamental ideas that are drawn from the larger trends prevalent in American decorative arts of the period. This chest of drawers is beautifully painted with rosettes, tulips, birds, tiny leaping animals, compass stars, and a border of stamped rosettes.

Many of the decorative motifs on Mayer's chests relate to printed *Taufscheine* (birth and baptismal certificates), but his design vocabulary also is tied to one of the preeminent families in the region, through the marriage of Mayer's daughter Elizabeth to Jared Stiehly,

the son of Reverend Isaac Stiehly. Reverend Stiehly was a popular pastor, gravestone carver, and *Scherenschnitte* (paper cutting) and fraktur artist. An examination of Stiehly's stone carving reveals a stacked arrangement of shaped cartouches with rosettes bordering each side, ideas borrowed by Mayer.

—Stacy C. Hollander

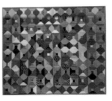

**Log Cabin Quilt,
Courthouse Steps Variation**

According to tradition, this quilt was made by a male tailor who reportedly used remnants of satin and velvet linings for what was probably a parlor throw. Samuel Steinberger was one of the immigrants who poured into New York ports of entry from areas of eastern Europe in the last decades of the nineteenth century and early years of the twentieth. Many of these immigrants were Jews fleeing mounting oppression in the 1880s. A large number were trained in the textile trades and congregated in a small area on the Lower East Side, which quickly became New York City's first predominantly Jewish neighborhood and one of the most heavily populated areas of the country. The New York City Directory for 1900 and the New York State census for the same year list a "Sam'l Steinberger, tailor," living at 352 East Third Street in Manhattan. According to the census, both Steinberger and his wife, Sarah, were born in Hungary—Samuel in April 1865 and Sarah in January 1870. Steinberger immigrated to America in 1884, and he and Sarah married in 1889. Directory listings through 1925 show "Sam'l" and his family at a number of different addresses in Manhattan and the Bronx until 1934, when Sarah is listed as a widow living in the Bronx with her daughter.

Steinberger's quilt is an unusual variation of the Courthouse Steps pattern. Atypical changes in color and fabric—the substitution of a light color where a dark would be expected, for instance—give the quilt a visual unpredictability that is different from the regularity usually associated with Log Cabins.

—Stacy C. Hollander

Tall Case Clock

———————— ◎ ————————

Until the discovery of this clock, Johannes Spitler had been known to researchers only by the initials "j.SP." Not only does this clock provide Spitler's name spelled in full, but it also reveals significant connections between his visual vocabulary and that of his neighbor, fraktur artist Jacob Strickler. Assumptions have always been made in the study of American Germanic and Swiss furniture, particularly in regard to Pennsylvania examples, that some designs on painted furniture were derived from fraktur drawing; rarely does such compelling evidence exist, however, as it does in the documented visual communication between Spitler and Strickler.

Indeed, the household in which the case clock descended possessed an unparalleled wealth of material relating to both men, including ten fraktur writing and drawing specimens by Strickler, nine of which are now in the collection of the Abby Aldrich Rockefeller Folk Art Museum in Williamsburg, Virginia. The tenth specimen, a fraktur with inverted heart by Jacob Strickler found later in the same household, accompanied this clock when it passed from the family in 1978. These fraktur, or perhaps a single fraktur like Strickler's complex 1794 *Zierschrift* (decorative writing), now in the Henry Francis du Pont Winterthur Museum in Winterthur, Delaware, clearly provided Spitler with the source for motifs displayed on the clock he personalized for Strickler. The two distinctive floral blossoms rising from inverted heart "bulbs" on the sides of the hood segment of the clock, the harlequin zigzag pattern variation on the waist of the clock, and indeed the precise style of the fraktur script of the inscription itself on the raised panel on front are all copied from Strickler fraktur. The crescent-moon faces on the sides, on the other hand, appear on no other recorded Spitler furniture, or Strickler fraktur, for that matter.

All elements on this clock are painted in Spitler's standard palette. The only other recorded clock by Spitler with surviving decoration is inscribed "1800 / j SP No 2"; it has a more conventional, architecturally inspired form with a broken-arched hood, defined waist, and a base with bracket feet. The coffinlike Strickler/ Spitler clock, however, is rather unconventional in construction, including a labor-intensive technique in which the raised panels in the door and the inscription panel above the door are actually carved in relief rather than inset in framework.

—Donald R. Walters

Round Box with Heart Decorations

———————— ◎ ————————

This shallow round box, similar in form to bentwood pantry boxes, is one of sixteen pieces by George Robert Lawton that descended in his family. The incised decoration on the top derives from compass designs and bears a striking resemblance to the radial motifs found on a painted chest from the Hadley area of Massachusetts. But it also relates strongly to the configuration of dartboards. The game of darts has a long history in Europe and America and originally was played on slices of wood cut from the trunk of a tree. The natural rings and radial cracks provided the playing and scoring areas, and ultimately evolved into the board with which we are familiar today, based on a numbering system known as the "clock." The scoring areas are delineated by wire rings called "spiders," which separate the board into three rings and the central bull's-eye. The spots that fill the decorated areas of the box also resemble the marks left by darts in the surface of the playing board.

—Stacy C. Hollander

USEFUL INFORMATION, INSTRUCTIONS & YARN CONVERSION CHART

by Karyn Gerhard

MATERIALS & GENERAL INFORMATION

❋ ❋ ❋

CANVAS

The choice of canvas is a matter of personal preference. There are three standard types of canvas:

- **MONO:** Single-thread canvas with an over-and-under weave. Mono canvases come in a wide range of sizes.

- **INTERLOCK:** Threads twisted at the intersection so they lock together. Interlock comes in medium and large gauges, making it a particular favorite for making rugs.

- **PENELOPE:** A double-thread canvas, with two threads for every gauge. The threads can be split to work petit point and standard needlepoint in the same piece.

Each has their particular advantages and disadvantages. For example, interlock canvas has a tendency to pull out of shape more quickly than the other types of canvas, while Penelope, although stronger (because you are needlepointing over two threads), can make you feel cross-eyed if you are not used to it. I prefer mono canvas, which is sturdy and holds its shape well.

Canvas size is determined by its gauge—in other words, the number of stitches to an inch (2.5 cm) of canvas. For example, 14-gauge canvas has 14 stitches to the inch (2.5 cm). Although the gauge count is given for each design, you can stitch the projects on any gauge canvas you wish, though of course the finished size will differ. You can easily determine what size your pattern will be by dividing the number of stitches (given in the pattern legend) by the number of the gauge. Consider, for example, the Cross River Cushion, page 58. At present, this is worked on a 12-gauge canvas, resulting in a pillow that is 14 x 14" (35.5 x 35.5 cm). If you want to use 14-gauge canvas, and want to know the finished size, you would divide the stitches (168) by 14: your pillow will be 12 x 12" (30.5 x 30.5 cm).

Interlock and mono canvases come in a range of colors but are most readily available in white and ecru. If you are working on something that tends to have mostly dark colors, it is better, though not necessary, to work on a brown or dark-colored canvas to lessen the appearance of any show-through.

YARN

The choice of yarn used for the projects in this book is sometimes the result of my own preference or because it is a more practical decision. If a piece calls for Paternayan wool, but the shiny look of DMC Pearl Cotton is more to your liking or would work better with your décor, then by all means use it. Take into consideration how the piece is going to be used. For example, Paternayan wool for the Packard Footstool, page 68, because it provides the durability needed.

When purchasing yarn it is best to get all of the yarn you need from the same dye lot. Yarn colors can vary from lot to lot, sometimes slightly and other times rather noticeably, so to prevent any problems down the road get all of your supplies from the same place and at one time. The conversion chart on page 142 will help you determine the colors you need, but keep in mind that color comparisons are approximate.

The following yarns are used in this book:

- **PERSIAN WOOL:** Three strands twisted together. The strands can be separated and used in varying thicknesses or color combinations to cover the desired canvas. Depending on the number of strands used, Persian wool can be used in all gauges of canvas.

- **TAPESTRY WOOL:** A single, twisted strand of wool. Because it cannot be separated, tapestry wool should not be used for any canvas smaller than 12 gauge.

- **COTTON FLOSS:** Six-stranded twisted cotton with a sheen that can be separated into strands and combined with other colors or used in varying thicknesses to cover the canvas.

- **PEARL COTTON:** A single, twisted strand with a high sheen. It comes in two weights, 3 and 5 (the higher the number, the thinner the strand). Pearl 3 is recommended for gauge counts of 12 to 14; Pearl 5 is recommended for petit point and gauges 16 count and higher. If you wish to use Pearl on a 10-gauge canvas, double the thread. Pearl is not recommended for anything larger than 10-gauge canvas.

NEEDLES

Tapestry needles should always be used for needlepoint projects; the eye is large enough to thread the thickest wool, and the blunt tip won't split the thread (or puncture your fingers). Needle sizes are numbered; the larger the number, the smaller the needle. Needle sizes are given for each project, but a general rule of thumb is that a size 20 needle is best for 10- to 14-gauge canvases; a size 22 needle is best for 16- to 18-gauge canvases.

FRAMES

The use of a stretcher or scroll frame is also a personal preference. Although a frame will keep your canvas taut and may save some distortion and time in blocking the piece afterward, it makes it nearly impossible to travel with your needlework. So if your tension is uniform and not too tight, a frame is not an absolute necessity. I prefer not to work with a frame so that I can take my project with me wherever I go. There are many different types of frames from which to choose, including standing floor frames, lap frames, and stretcher frames, which are available at your local craft store or online.

GETTING STARTED

❋ ❋ ❋

PREPARING THE CANVAS

Be sure to purchase enough canvas so that you have at least 2 to 3" (5–7.5 cm) of overage on each side of the project. The size of the canvas recommended for each project allows for this overage. The extra canvas will be trimmed when the project is finished. Because canvas has a tendency to fray, it is important to cover the raw edges with masking tape or white artist's tape before you start stitching. Set the canvas on half of the tape and fold the tape over the edge to cover it completely.

Before starting to stitch (or mounting the canvas on a frame, if you are using one), mark the center of your canvas. Fold the canvas in half horizontally, then vertically, and mark the fold point very lightly, preferably with a fabric pen (a pencil may smudge the yarn). It is best to always start stitching your patterns from this center point so that you don't accidentally run out of canvas before running out of pattern.

WORKING FROM A CHART

Many people are intimidated by working from a chart, but it is actually easier than working from a pattern printed on canvas, where a color may fall between two holes. There is no confusion with a chart because each block of color on the chart represents one stitch, thus 6 blocks of green, for example, equals 6 stitches. For larger areas, I find it easiest to count and stitch the outer edge of the area and then fill it in with the basketweave stitch.

Each chart in this book is noted with arrows indicating the center of the pattern; it is always best to start in the middle and work your way out. Begin with one color and work as much as you can with that color; in this way it will act as an anchor and make it easier to navigate your way around the rest of the chart.

STITCHES
❋ ❋ ❋

Needlepoint is based on one stitch, but there are many variations for creating beautiful and unusual patterns. I prefer to use these variations in large areas of background, but once you familiarize yourself with the various stitches in this book, you can experiment and use them any way you like.

THE BASICS:
TENT & BASKETWEAVE

TENT

The *tent* stitch is the most basic needlepoint stitch. Although it is highly versatile, tent stitch should not be used for background work because it tends to pull the canvas out of shape. There are two techniques for tent stitch: *continental* and *half-cross*. Both techniques are worked right to left—the half-cross by making short vertical stitches in the back and the continental by making longer, slanting stitches.

BASKETWEAVE

Basketweave gets its name from the over-and-under weave it creates on the back of the canvas and is best used for covering large areas. Not only is it durable, but there is less pull on the canvas when using basketweave. The individual stitch is a tent stitch (hence the reason it is sometimes called a *diagonal tent stitch*), but instead of working in

a horizontal row, you work on the *diagonal* rows, starting in the top left of the area to be covered, going from upper left to lower right, and then back up again.

THE VARIATIONS:
CHECKERBOARD, GOBELIN, BYZANTINE, SATIN & T-STITCH

CHECKERBOARD

The checkerboard stitch is basically square blocks of tent stitches going in different directions. You work one block of stitches facing left, and the next block facing right. The effect is subtle when the background is all one color, and has a greater checkerboard pattern if you use more than one color for the background. The number of stitches in the square block is up to you, but the larger the piece, the larger the blocks should be, though to achieve the best effect, a block of stitches should be no more than 1" (2.5 cm) square.

GOBELIN

The gobelin stitch is basically an elongated version of tent stitch, going over two or three holes (depending on the effect desired) instead of just one. It can be worked diagonally or vertically. For an even-textured finish, make sure that the yarn does not twist and lies flat.

BYZANTINE

To create the diagonal stepped effect of the Byzantine stitch, work gobelin stitches in alternating horizontal and vertical rows. In order to have an even background effect, it is important to make sure each diagonal row is continuous, from the top to the bottom. To achieve this, count through the decorative pattern and pick up Byzantine stitch where the background begins again (you can see this around the branches and butterflies on the Bird of Paradise Wedge Pillow, page 48).

SATIN

Satin stitch is really an embroiderer's filler stitch but can easily be adapted for needlepoint. This stitch is great for working curves, such as the leaves in the Floral Purse, page 76. The satin stitch is somewhat like the gobelin stitch in that you are going across two or three holes, but the difference is that the stitches radiate out from a single hole. In order to achieve a smooth shading effect, stagger the stitches.

T-STITCH

The T-stitch is a variation using the basic continental stitch in alternating slants. Because every other canvas intersection is not stitched, the canvas is partially exposed, giving a light, lacelike appearance. This stitch is most effective in background or large decorative areas and is even more impressive if you use a colored canvas. Working in diagonal rows (as you do with basketweave stitch), first stitch all of the rows in one direction, skipping every other canvas intersection and every other row, then stitch the skipped rows in the alternate direction. Make sure to hide your traveling thread underneath existing stitches so that it doesn't interfere with the airiness of the pattern.

STARTING TO STITCH

No matter which kind of yarn used for a project, the length of yarn should always be the same. The ideal length should not exceed 18" (45.5cm); if you use anything longer, the yarn will fray from being pulled through the canvas too many times. Unlike embroidery, you never want to have knots in the back of your canvas. In order to anchor your yarn, make a knot at the end of the yarn. Push the yarn through from the top of the canvas, 1" (2.5cm) away from where the actual first stitch will be so that the knot is on the top left of the canvas. Then come up from the bottom and make your first stitch and stitch back toward the knot, covering the yarn on the back with your stitches as you go. When you get to the knot, cut it off—your first length of yarn is now anchored.

To anchor a new thread in a section that has already been worked, pass the needle under a few of the already-worked stitches on the back of the canvas. When you come to the end of a thread, finish it off by running it underneath a few of the nearby stitches on the back of the canvas and cutting it as close to the canvas as possible for a clean finish. If you leave too much yarn on the back you run the risk of pulling it through when you continue stitching, either with the same color or a different one. If the yarn starts to twist while you are working, stop and hold the canvas upside down so that the thread can dangle and untwist itself.

WHEN THINGS GO WRONG

There is nothing worse than finishing a large section and realizing that you skipped a stitch or a row and the whole pattern is off. When this happens, there is usually little you can do except to find out where the mistake was made and carefully pick out the yarn back to that place and start again. If you have only missed by one stitch, and it doesn't throw off the entire pattern, you can leave it and just pick up stitching in the correct place—no one will know!

To pull out stitches, it is best to take a seam ripper or small scissors to snip the stitches from the back, then pick the cut yarn out with tweezers or your needle. Do not try to pull the yarn out and reuse it; in most cases, the yarn will be too frayed or twisted. Be careful not to snip the canvas when cutting stitches. That said, if you do happen to cut the canvas, or in the unlikely event that a canvas breaks, it can be easily fixed. Cut out a small piece of canvas from your overage and place it behind the damaged piece of canvas, lining up the meshes. Continue stitching through both pieces of canvas.

To avoid the headache of having to rip out stitches, the best piece of advice I can give is a paraphrase of the old carpenter's adage: count twice, stitch once. I am obsessive about constantly checking my stitches. While you are stitching, occasionally stop and check your work to make sure it is lining up with the graph as well as with the other colors on the canvas.

FINISHING INSTRUCTIONS
❋ ❋ ❋

Professional finishers are the best route for blocking and finishing your needlepoint, especially for pieces that require using special equipment to finish them (such as a leather-stitching machine for a belt). The following instructions are for basic finishing.

BLOCKING

Whether or not you have used a frame while stitching, your canvas will have to be blocked in order to bring it back to its true shape before mounting. For this you will need a stretcher frame, carpet tacks, a T-square, and a lot of patience. (You can also use a board that is slightly larger than your finished piece.) Do not cut off the canvas overage before you have blocked your piece. Place the canvas face-down on the board or stretcher frame, line up one side of your canvas and tack it in place. Dampen the back of the canvas with water (either with a sponge or misting bottle), being careful not to completely soak it. Pull and tack the remaining sides until your piece is very taut and all of the sides are even, re-wetting the canvas as needed. Once all of the sides are secured, let it dry completely (this may take up to a few days). If you find that it is still not completely square when you take it off the stretcher, repeat the process.

SIMPLE BACKING

This technique can be used for most pieces, from a curtain tieback to a pincushion or pillow.

Trim the canvas overage to ½" (13 mm) all the way round. Cut the fabric ½" (13 mm) wider than the canvas (for the seam allowance). Place the two pieces together, right-side in (that is, the backs of both pieces should be facing out), and pin them together. Stitch three sides and part of the fourth, stitching between the first and second rows of the pattern, to ensure that no blank canvas appears at the seams. Turn the piece right-side out and slip stitch the rest of the edge closed. For cushions, insert the pillow form before stitching the fourth side closed.

BRICK COVER

First, cover the brick in muslin or calico, wrapping it like a gift and basting the edges closed. Trim the canvas to ¾" (2 cm) all the way round. Fold the canvas, wrong-side out, and stitch together the corner seams. Trim away the excess canvas to ½" (13 mm) and press the seam open. Turn the piece right-side out and insert the brick. Lace the bottom, using leftover yarn or heavy thread, going side to side and top to bottom, to enclose the brick. Pull the yarn very taught so the canvas cannot shift. Cut a piece of heavy furnishing fabric ½" (13 mm) larger than the bottom of the brick (for seam allowance). Fold the seam allowance, press, then baste the fabric to the bottom of the brick.

FRAMING ART

The simplest way to frame art is to just leave it on the stretcher canvas and either find a frame to fit or build a frame around it, using individual frame pieces. If you wish to hang the piece without a frame, you will need thin 2-ounce (56.7 g) batting and heavy, upholstery-type fabric. Cut the batting to ½" (13 mm) smaller than the original piece and baste it to the wrong side of the canvas. Put the canvas and fabric together, right-side in, and stitch three sides and part of the fourth. Turn it right-side out and stitch the rest of the edge closed. You can then hang this on a dowel hanger.

PICTURE FRAME

You will need heavy-duty masking tape and two pieces of thick cardboard, each the size of the finished piece, one with a hole cut in the center, for your picture. Trim the overage canvas to 1½" (3.8 cm). Also cut out the unworked canvas in the middle, leaving the same overage amount. Trim the corners of the outer edge of overage diagonally and make diagonal cuts in the center overage so that you can fold these pieces back. Place the piece of cardboard with the hole on the back of the canvas. Fold the outer right-hand edge of the canvas over the cardboard and tape into place (leave the other outer edges free). Fold and tape all of the inner edges. Place the second piece of cardboard on top of this; fold over the other three sides and tape into place. Slide the picture into place through the open side.

JOINING PIECES OF CANVAS

This technique can be used for the Compass Star Eyeglass Case and Floral Purse, if you are stitching both front and back pieces. Fold the edges of the canvas, making sure that the holes of the overage canvas are lined up with the stitched side. With the right sides facing out, stitch the two pieces together using a half-cross stitch with the same color yarn as the edge (or a corresponding color).

YARN CONVERSION CHART
❋ ❋ ❋

The following chart converts DMC cotton, Paternayan Persian wool, and Anchor tapestry wool. Note that DMC Cotton Floss and Pearl Cotton share the same item numbers. Where two numbers are given, such as DMN 415 (647), this means that either are acceptable, although the first color is the best match.

All yarns come in different skein lengths, so keep this in mind if you are converting to a type of yarn other than what is suggested.

DMC Pearl 3: 16.4 yards (15 m)
DMC Pearl 5: 27 yards (24.7 m)
DMC Cotton Floss: 8.7 yards (8 m)
Paternayan wool: 8 yards (7.3 m)
Anchor wool: 11 yards (110.6 m)

YARN CONVERSION CHART

✳ ✳ ✳

DMC	PATERNAYAN	ANCHOR
BLANC	260	8000
ECRU	262	8006
—	101	—
—	102	—
—	202	—
—	324	8522
—	401	
—	417	9426
—	463	9656
—	464	9654
—	465	
3810	533	8900
—	551	8690
—	850	—
169	—	—
221	870 (890)	8264
302	—	
304	969 (968)	1006
310	220	9800
312	501 (502)	8792
315 (221)	921	8510
319 (520)	600	9022
320	602	9018
321	970	8216
322	503	8790
334	503	—
335	—	—
336	571	8636
349	841	8216
350	842	8198
351	863	8258
352	844	8258
353	845	—
356	482	8348
413	200	9764
415 (647)	203	8892
433	411	9452
434	412	8064
435	495	9448
436	497	9444
437	362	9786
469	692	9204
519	504	8776
543	475	9632
601	960	8456
604	963	8452
632	481	7167
676	734	8040
712	327	8838
729	733 (815)	8022
730	651	9292
734	653	9274
738	498	9522
739	499	9442
740	812	—
741	813	8154
742	814	8124
743	703	8136
746	755	8032
758	834	8254
783	732	8102
798	543	8690
799	544	(136)
801	—	9410
803	—	—
806	583	8820
814	967	8404
815	901	8402
816 (3687)	900	8220
817	970	8216
820	540	8794
823	571	8694
824	550	8632
828	506 (555)	9159
838	471	9598
841	—	9638
842	405	9324
898	430	9642
906	697	9156
907	634	9114
911	621	9102
920	881	1004
921	831	1003
922	—	1003
924	532 (534)	8882
927	515	8894
928	525	8872
930	511	1035
931	512	1034
934	450	9080
937	—	9204
950 (945)	875	8342
951	493	1010
977	724	8060
977	723	1002
986	610	9008
996	—	—
3011	651	9216
3012	652	9214
3013	695	9256
3752 (932)	514	8832
3325	505	8796
3347	693	9174
3740	—	8548
3746	341	1030
3750 (3760)	510	8740
3772	484	9598
3773	486	1008
3809	581	8822
3810	533	8900
3820	702	8022
3822	727	8016
3823	756	8034
3826	—	9556

SOURCES

✳ ✳ ✳

Although the sources listed below are based in New York, feel free to explore local stores in your own area or contact these suppliers through their websites.

Aphrodisia Herb Shoppe
264 Bleecker Street
New York, New York 10012
phone 212.989.6440; fax 212.989.8027
www.aphrodisiaherbshoppe.com
Good source for herbs or fragrance beads
for sachets or paperweights.

B&J Fabrics
525 Seventh Avenue, 2nd floor
New York, New York 10018
phone 212.354.8150; toll-free 866.354.8150
www.bandjfabrics.com
A well-organized fabric store with high-quality goods
that just about has anything you could hope to find.
Tends to be pricey.

Diamint Upholstery
336 East 59th Street
New York, New York 10022
phone 212.715.0903; fax 212.715.0904
www.diamintupholstery.com
The family-run business excels in custom upholstery,
drapes, and furniture. Diamint completed the Packard
Footstool in this book.

Bespoke, Resources for Interiors
25 East 67th Street, Suite 9AB
New York, New York 10021
phone 212.734.4800
This custom furniture shop produces, among other
things, the footstool on page 68. Ask for Susan Hager.

**House of Heydenryk: Custom and
Antique Frames**
610 West 26th Street, Suite 305
New York, New York 10001
phone 212.206.9611; fax 212.206.9615
www.heydenryk.com
For more than 150 years, Heydenryk has been a top-
notch provider of handmade reproduction frames,
antique frames, and original designs. Contact Laurie
Luczak, who is knowledgeable and always helpful.
Heydenryk frames were used for the Weathervane
Silhouette and Hannah Carter Tapestry in this book.

M&J Trimming
1008 Sixth Avenue
New York, New York 10018
phone 212.204.9595; toll-free 800.9.MJTRIM
www.mjtrim.com
Terrific selection of trims, ribbons, tassels, handles, clasps,
buttons, and other closures. It's best to know what you
want or else give yourself time to browse around.

Martin Albert Interiors, Inc.
9 East 19th Street
New York, New York 10003
phone 212.673.8000; toll-free 800.525.4637;
fax 212.673.8006
www.martinalbert.com
Rene Cortas is the person to see—he's kind and will
work with you on completing a needlework project.
Martin Albert made the Bird of Paradise Wedge Pillow
in this book.

Mood Designer Fabrics
225 West 37th Street, 3rd floor
New York, New York 10018
phone 212.730.5003; fax 212.221.1932
www.moodfabrics.com
If you watch *Project Runway* or *The Apprentice*, then you
know about Mood. It's an amazing trove of fabrics and
trims on three floors, best suited to someone who is
self-reliant and loves to root around for the perfect textile.

Purl Patchwork
147 Sullivan Street
New York, New York 10012
phone 212.420.8798
www.purlsoho.com
A perfect gem, located in SoHo; I looked forward
to my every visit. Although the fabrics are ostensibly
for quilting, I found the selection ideal for the folk art
needlework projects. What's more, you can buy as little
as ¼ yard (23 cm), which is sometimes all you need. It
bears mentioning that the website is simply beautiful
and easy to navigate.

Rita's Needlepoint
150 East 79th Street
New York, New York 10021
phone 212.737.8613; fax 212.737.8097
www.ritasneedlepoint.com
As they say on their website: *"Nous Parlons Français; Wir
Sprechen Deutsch; Hablamos Español."* Rita's does its best
to work with one and all, including custom work and
special hand lettering and designs by Rita herself. What
makes the shop so superb is the incredible selection of
canvases   many of them unique to Rita's, especially
those from France—and variety of yarn. Just as varied
are the many novelty items and projects available, such
as canvas bags, hand-painted porcelain boxes, or wallets.
Christmas is a big deal here, from stockings to tree
ornaments.

"Regulars" make up a large part of the clientele,
in part because of the extremely helpful and patient
staff. Barbara Riering is the majordomo and everyone's
favorite. With few exceptions, Rita's provided the
finishing services on the projects in this book.

NEEDLEPOINT WEBSITES

American Needlepoint Guild, Inc.
www.needlepoint.org

DMC Corporation
www.dmc-usa.com

The National Needle Arts Association
www.tnna.org

Needlepointers.com
www.needlepointers.com

ABOUT THE PHOTOGRAPHER

Annie Schlechter is a native New Yorker who
has been doing photography since 1998. She's
photographed books for Jonathan Adler and Real
Simple, and her clients include Domino, Aero, Pottery
Barn, the Neue Gallerie, and World of Interiors.

ACKNOWLEDGMENTS

>>>>>>>>>✳<<<<<<<<

I've been an editor of art and illustrated books for a long while, and some years ago one of my authors insisted that I learn to do needlepoint. No way, I told her, I can't sew or cut a straight line. But she was persistent, and soon afterward a little bag appeared at my office with all the stuff a rookie needlepointer would need. I've been hooked ever since. So my first thanks are to Bunny Koppelman, author and friend. The canvas I was given came from Rita's Needlepoint, located on the Upper East Side of New York. When I was working on a project, I was often at the shop asking for advice, and bless those women there because they always made me feel welcome, especially Barbara Riering, the co-owner. Over the years Barbara and I became friendly, and it was Barbara with whom I concocted the idea for this book. Her creative ideas and advice are evident in the overall shape of this book and in the completed projects. The staff at Rita's, Kandace Merric and Jennifer B. Smith, have always been kind to me and are endowed with limitless patience. Rita Klein, who opened the boutique in 1976, adheres to the highest standards of excellence—it became a goal of mine to get a smile of approval from her whenever I would bring in my needlework. Significantly for this book, Rita's Needlepoint partnered with me in doing the finishing of the canvases here, although I fear that for a time I became what is known in the world of Edward Gorey as "the doubtful guest."

If Barbara was my right hand, then Karyn Gerhard was my left hand in this venture. She was also the artist par excellence who charted and designed the projects here. Indeed, Karyn stitched nearly every single canvas, which means that she has chalked up over a million stitches, surely a record of sorts somewhere. Karyn and I first met when we were both working at Harry N. Abrams Publishers, where she was known for being an ardent needlepointer. Karyn was consistently faithful to the objects from the American Folk Art Museum that she adapted to canvas, and her instructions on how to work with various materials and such are an invaluable section unto themselves in the book.

Blessings on the American Folk Art Museum, in particular deputy director Linda Dunne, for allowing us to develop this book based on their superb collection. I also wish to thank Tanya Heinrich, director of publications, and Mareike Grover, managing editor, in the museum's Publications Department for their help and contributions to this book.

A city like New York has such great resources, and there are many suppliers here that deserve recognition. Although a detailed list of sources is on the preceding page, I want to single out a few people and places. Surely one of the kindest men to be found in the Garment District is Marlon López, at M&J Trimming. Not only is Marlon the go-to person for the M&J staff, he was my go-to person as well, and I benefited from his gracious help and advice. Laurie Luczak, at House of Heydenryk, is blessed with a sunny disposition and a keen sense of the framer's art, both attributes which I esteem. Silvia Gonzalez at Diamint Upholstery runs the shop with a smile and decades of experience. And I spent many happy hours looking at fabrics with Jill Hoffman at Mood Designer Fabrics.

Annie Schlechter, who took the interiors photographs in this book, deserves a gold star beside her name. Not only is she creative, she's funny. Funny should be a job requirement in every collaboration for it makes the difference between work being like play, or like, well, work. My thanks also to Kristy Workman, who assisted on the photo shoot with diligence and care.

Thank you always to my ever-devoted and smart agent, Alice F. Martell; to Elizabeth V. Warren and Irwin H. Warren for their peerless taste and advice; and to Carlene Harwick and Jacqui Clarkson of the National Academy of Needlearts.

At Potter Craft, a warm thanks to my wonderful editor, Erin Slonaker, and to Christina Schoen and Jennifer Graham in the editorial department; and also to Chi Ling Moy, art director; La Tricia Watford, designer; and Rosy Ngo, editorial director.

Although I began this note by explaining my current involvement in needlepoint, the real inspiration goes back decades. My paternal grandmother, after whom I was named and revere to this day, was an accomplished needlepointer. Her projects ranged from the small 'n' easy to the ambitious and complex: bookmarks, tennis racquet covers, footstools, and intricately stitched seat cushions for her dining room chairs, all eight of them. By that measure, I've got a long way to go.

Ruth Peltason
NEW YORK, NEW YORK